MW01256398

80 PERCENT LUCK, 20 PERCENT SKILL
My Life as a WWII Navy Ferry Pilot

Ralph T. Alshouse

Black Rose Writing | Texas

©2023 by Ralph T. Alshouse

All rights reserved. No part of this book may be reproduced, stored in a retrieval system or transmitted in any form or by any means without the prior written permission of the publishers, except by a reviewer who may quote brief passages in a review to be printed in a newspaper, magazine or journal.

The author grants the final approval for this literary material.

First printing

The opinions and characterizations in this book are those of the author and do not necessarily represent the official position of the U.S. Navy

Unless otherwise credited, all photographs of aircraft are file photographs. Photographs of Ralph Alshouse are from family archives.

This written work is registered with the U.S. Copyright Office. Photographs contained herein, including the cover photograph, are specifically excluded from said copyright.

ISBN: 978-1-68513-341-2
PUBLISHED BY BLACK ROSE WRITING
www.blackrosewriting.com

Printed in the United States of America
Suggested Retail Price (SRP) $19.95

80 Percent Luck, 20 Percent Skill is printed in Bookman Old Style

*As a planet-friendly publisher, Black Rose Writing does its best to eliminate unnecessary waste to reduce paper usage and energy costs, while never compromising the reading experience. As a result, the final word count vs. page count may not meet common expectations.

To My Children

Official Navy photograph of Ensign Alshouse, 1943

80 PERCENT LUCK,
20 PERCENT SKILL

INTRODUCTION

It was a chance encounter meeting Ralph Alshouse at a Veteran Affairs Appreciation Dinner in the little town of Seymour, Iowa. I didn't expect to see anyone wearing a ballcap with faded gold letters "WWII" on the front, or the gold wings of a Naval Aviator pinned on the side, but when this lightly bearded man, about six-foot tall and thin as a rail, entered the community center, I stood up and waved at him like we were long-lost friends. He acknowledged me with a wave and a smile, and he made his way to where I was sitting.

I scanned the room to see if there were any other gold Naval Aviator wings pinned on hats. It seemed the WWII war hero walking toward me and I were probably the only Naval Aviators in the room. And I had no idea what to expect.

His hearing wasn't too good, even with hearing aids, but we eventually found out we had common experiences. Ralph Alshouse flew bent-wing F-4 or FG Corsairs and other airplanes during the hot war, and I flew bent-wing F-4 Phantoms during the cold war. He said he loved flying the F-4; I absolutely agreed.

Ralph's stories were infinitely more interesting than mine. Ralph was all transmit, I was all receive, and I did not care in the least. He asked if I ever had an F-4 on fire—

I said my F-4 had two afterburning engines—some part of my jet was always on fire! We howled! He asked if I ever had a dead stick landing—I said no, that if my training aid ever quit doing her job of blowing fire out the back end, I would have just ejected and sent her back to the taxpayers. We howled again! Then Ralph asked if I ever got a "Dear John."

I said, "No."

Ralph said, "You lucked out!" I laughed so hard.

We probably carried on like frat boys; the VA Office Director even gave us the evil eye. A look that implied, *Can't take you boys anywhere!*

I told my wife that after being out of the cockpit for over 35 years, I just had one of the most remarkable experience in memory. I said, "I can still remember the few emergencies I had as a pilot, but I will never forget that evening with Ralph Alshouse."

Several months later, sitting at a table in an Allerton, Iowa convenience store having breakfast with a bunch of farmers, Ralph walked in with a VRF-2 ballcap. The farmers were deferential and pleasant to the old war hero. Ralph sat a different table, and I got up and sat across from him.

He remembered me from the VA dinner. We had chatted for about a half-hour when he said he had put together a binder for his children of his memories as a ferry pilot. It began when he was an eleven-year-old Iowa farm boy and saw a Cub for the very first time. Ralph continued; he became a Navy Cadet, then went to flight school, and on to support the war effort with a Navy ferry squadron, VRF-2.

I learned Ralph took new planes from factories in the U.S. and Canada to awaiting carriers off the east and west coasts. He had amassed over fifteen-hundred flight hours.

When he said he had the weather or thirteen aircraft fail him during that time of the war, 1943-1945, some of which he had to dead stick the landings, I was simply dumbfounded. Without sufficient altitude to parachute, he rode the airplanes with dead motors or on fire down to the ground—anywhere he could land. Ralph said he was told he holds the military record for aircraft that essentially quit running after takeoff or being forced down because of adverse weather, without getting significantly injured or killed.

He said at one point, he had made six trips from Columbus, Ohio to California in seven days. Simply incredible.

99 years old... thirteen forced landing in the most harrowing of conditions... and lived to talk about it. That was simply incredible on so many levels. No wonder he was in such good spirits.

I sat there, speechless; it was such an amazing claim. I explained I was spending my retirement writing novels about airplanes, and in my world of flying jets, walking away from thirteen forced landings, dead stick landings, aircraft on fire, whatever Ralph experienced as a ferry pilot, was a unique achievement. Since he had recorded some of those events for his children, I asked if he would allow me to look at his binder of stories to see if he had enough material for a book.

He considered it and stated he would pay me for my time. I was just going to look.

I learned so much about Lt Ralph Alshouse by scanning his typewritten pages, converting them, and copying them onto a file. I found it sad that he's the last surviving member of his WWII VRF-2 squadron. Ralph explained they used to have reunions every few years until his former squadron mates became unable to travel. He and his squadron mates used to exchange Christmas cards with each other, and when he didn't receive a single Christmas card last year; he knew he was the last, that there was no one to exchange cards with any longer.

That's when significant leakage occurred around my old fighter-pilot, Mk 2 eyeballs.

Ralph is still very sharp; he drives, plays nine holes on Wednesday—weather permitting. He's all into nutrition and seven of his eight children are still alive. One daughter edited his stories before we submitted them for publication.

It has been a treat to meet this war hero every week and have breakfast with him.

He is the last of his kind.

It's been an absolute honor and privilege knowing Lieutenant Ralph Alshouse, USNR, Ret.

Mark A. Hewitt
Captain, USMC, Ret.

Ralph Alshouse, 1941

PRE-FLIGHT

My First Airplane

Why would an Iowan farm boy ever want to be a Navy pilot?

In the spring of 1935, when I was eleven, my father sent me to cultivate a soybean field on the far side of our rented farm. Like most days on the farm, I harnessed a team of horses, then hitched them to a row walking-cultivator. Walking bare-footed in the soft, warm soil behind a cultivator, driving a team of horses was fun and challenging, although it can get a little old when my day after day chores turn into weeks.

But one day was unlike any other in my short life. My boredom was shattered by a noise like an engine. It was coming from the air. I stopped the team and looked around. It was a yellow machine in the air, the first airplane I had ever seen. I had only read about airplanes. It circled, then landed in the neighbor's hay field just across from the line fence I was cultivating. I thought, this must be the new landlord, because the farm next to ours had gone through foreclosure last year.

I stood quietly, holding on the horse's bridles, watching the airplane as it stopped. Two men in business suits climbed out of the airplane. A car arrived from the farmstead. The two men climbed into the car, leaving the airplane. The horses wandered off track, as I could not keep my eyes off of that airplane.

Eventually, I cultivated to the end of the soybean field, tied the team to the fence, and walked over to the airplane. To me, it was big, very big! It had two rubber wheels about the radius of a milk pail. At the tail area was a skid like a bobsled, only smaller. I walked around the airplane three times before deciding to touch it. It was smooth, but sounded hollow when I tapped the side of it with my fingers. I rubbed my hands along the side and over the wing. I peeked inside; all those dials and controls! Wow! I thought it must take a genius to know how to fly this machine. Years later, I learned it was a Piper Cub tail dragger.

File photograph of a Piper Cub

I was startled when my father spoke to me. He was cultivating corn in another field when he heard the airplane. He was concerned that my team might run away. We sat down in the shade of one wing, and my father explained to me more about airplanes. He had seen airplanes shoot each other down in France and Belgium while his 30th Division was breaking through the Hindenburg Line and into the Argonne Forest area. In his company of infantrymen, only Dad and two of his buddies lived through it.

The thought raced through my eleven-year-old mind, "If we ever get into another war, I wish to be an airplane pilot."

***

I was born left-handed. My mother and her sisters were of the firm conviction that any child born left-handed was next to sinful. They decided I must be changed to right-handed. According to my late Uncle Carl (one of mother's brothers), I was a challenge, but they accomplished their intent. The downside was I stuttered throughout grade school and high school. Some days, I could not even talk. Naturally, my grades reflected this by never getting an A or even a B grade. I got a few Cs, but not very many.

I graduated from high school in 1941, and World War II was declared in December 1941. I wanted to enlist right away, but my wise and thoughtful father refused to sign my enlistment papers.

The V5 Cadet Program

I started farming right out of high school and loved it. I could have easily been a draft dodger.

The local Lions Club in Oelwein, IA began recruiting local young men for the Navy Cadet Program. Twenty-five of us signed up in August 1942. I had wanted to enlist sooner, but Dad would not sign my papers until then. We were asked to board a Greyhound bus, which took us to Decorah, IA, for IQ and physical tests. Seven failed that level of testing. Two weeks later, eighteen of us boarded another bus for Minneapolis, MN for more testing. Nine of us were accepted by the Navy.

In September of 1942, I was sent to Eagle Grove Junior College. We rode an old school bus driven by one of our Navy cadets, named Voss, each morning to the Clarion Airport for flight preparation. All meals were at Eagle Grove and housing was on the third floor of one of their buildings. Afternoon classes were also at the Junior College. Our group was a little different, with ten Navy cadets and ten Army cadets. We got along great. Nick Nemo of VRF-2 was in this group. Iowa Governor George A. Wilson had his picture taken with us in late September.

I was the first to solo in our group on October 8, 1942, on a mostly sunny day with a 5-mph wind from the south. The airplane was a 65-horsepower Aeronca tail dragger, #31485. The solo time was 0740 to 0820. I had 2.4 hours of flight instruction.

Cadet Ralph Alshouse First Solo Flight, 1942

This picture was taken at the Clarion Airport with an Aeronca in the background. Army Cadet Rung from West Point, IA, on the left. Army Cadet Joe Hall from Cedar Rapids, IA on the right. The dog's name was Spinner. I was on top of the world.

Unforgettable Experiences
I Tried to Forget

I entered the Navy's pre-flight training course in Iowa City, IA. I was immediately assigned to the great sport of boxing. In high school, I never actually had a fight. My classmate, Dewy Rau, enjoyed the encounter of fist fighting. Each time I got close to an encounter, Dewy would always step in and take over.

The Navy instructors taught, showed, and trained us all in the art of boxing. We were divided into groups according to our weight. Each Monday, we were weighed and divided. The Golden Glove rules were explained and followed. Our boxing area had two regulation boxing rings, canvas mats, and exterior ropes. I had never seen one before.

After the first week of training, we were paired up to fight in the ring. Each ring had a referee, a timer, and bell. My first round was terrible. Blood from my nose was all over the mat. In the second round, my blood was all over both of us. This made me determined not to lose. In the third round, I caught my opponent with a solid right hook to his jaw, a knock out.

In the next match, I relearned what an upper cut was. It required three stitches after I won the fight. We were in the ring each day and each day more of my blood was dribbled on the mat. Each fight seemed to be harder than the one before. Apparently, all of us were getting better at boxing.

After the eighth or ninth match, I was pounded. At the end of the second round, one eye was almost swollen shut, my nose squirted blood and my left ear felt like it was partially ripped off. When the bell rang starting the third round, my opponent was pounding on my head when I saw an opening. I caught him with a half hook and a half upper cut with every ounce of energy I had. He went out through the ropes and laid on the floor. I thought I had killed him.

I climbed out and kneeled down beside him holding his head and shoulders. The referee yelled that he could not do the ten-count unless I was in the ring. Finally, the guy's eyes opened and I returned to the ring. After the ten-count, my opponent entered the ring, put his arm over my shoulders and said he would like to be my ring manager. I asked him what that was. He said every boxer had a hole in their boxing style and he could tell me what to look for in my opponents, that they all telegraph their deficiencies between the first and second rounds. That's when he told me he was the Illinois Golden Glove Champion.

We had 12 or 14 more fights before I won the 150-pound championship. The next Monday morning was weigh-in time. I had gained enough weight to be in the next weight class. My manager appeared to be so happy when we had 14 more fights. It always required two rounds for a knockout. The last one being for the championship again, and we went the full three rounds. The guy was so good I could not get a solid hit on him. I won the match by decision. The winner always gets bruised up. That match could have gone either way. I was so glad to hang up the boxing gloves.

Boxing was not a memorable event, but it was required to proceed. I was ready to start the Navy's flight school.

FLIGHT SCHOOL

First to Solo

I was sent to Eagle Grove and was the first of 20 to solo at the Clarion Airport. Some of us were sent to the University of Iowa at Iowa City for Pre-Flight training. Some were sent to Minneapolis, MN at Wold Chamberland Field for training in bi-wing training planes. We were in ground school one-half day and were flying the other half day.

Two of us completed all the training flights without a down check. A down check meant we had one more chance to do the maneuvers correctly or be busted out. Approximately 150 cadets started together, and about 30 or more failed. This is where I learned to help put a strait jacket on a fellow cadet after he killed another cadet in a landing accident in an N3N. This event is also how Maxie and I first become closer friends.

Maxie had graduated from college, and we had over four hours free each afternoon. The Navy had a policy that cadets were not to view our airplane wrecks. In our free time, when the weather was not conductive for flying or studying, Maxie and I would drift over to the aircraft repair facilities because we were of the mind to do whatever we could for the war effort, and we heard they were short-handed at the repair station. The Chief Petty Officer in charge started us at sweeping the floors, then operating metal turning lathes, and making universal joints used in hand-cranking airplane engines. Then the Chief had us help assemble aircraft engines from scratch. His Navy crew could only put two engines together a day, but they needed at least three. After several days of our help, the repair facility had been able to build three engines a day. A week went by when everything went ideally, and the decision was made that maybe we could assemble a fourth engine by the end of the day. We were almost done at quitting time, but everyone stayed at it to finish. Just when we finished, the lieutenant walked in catching Maxie and me red-handed!

The lieutenant ordered Maxie and me to meet with the Navy Skipper the next morning, at 0800, to be busted out. Neither of us slept very well that night, because we knew the rules. We were two sad, long-faced cadets the next morning when we stepped into the Skipper's Office. We snapped to attention and identified ourselves, then waited for the worst! After a couple of growls, and how rules should never be broken, he motioned for someone to come in, from a side door. It was the Chief Petty Officer. The Skipper said he understood we were doing a great job helping at the repair shop in our free time. The Skipper looked at Maxie, because he was older, and asked how soon we could get back to the repair shop? Maxie assured the Skipper we could get there on the double.

Pensacola Florida Naval Air Station

Cadet Wes Talbert and I were assigned the same room at the Pensacola Air Station. Immediately following our exchange of introductions, Wes requested my help in getting him up at reveille. The reason he said he needed help was the difficulty he had getting on his feet when the bugle sounded.

I promised him I would. Our room had two double deck bunks, a door, a window, and a sink. The first evening just before Taps, I washed up and set aside a glass of water.

The next morning, when the bugle sounded, I jumped up, while Wes was lying in his bunk "asleep." I applied the glass of water externally to his body, getting him up.

The second morning, Wes was slowly getting up when I applied a glass of water, while he was saying some unkind words.

The third morning, on the first note of reveille from the bugle, Wes applied a glass of water to my body with great laughter and glee!

With all the "water training" he was receiving, we were a little surprised that Wes was actually training to fly PB2Ys, flying boats.

Maxie

After completing our training at Wold Chamberland Field at Minneapolis, our group of cadets was sent by train to Pensacola, Florida. Arriving at the big Navy Flight Training Center, we were bussed out to the new, still under construction, Whiting Field. I marveled at the new barracks, classrooms, chow halls, runways, streets and roads.

We were flying larger training planes (SNJs). These were low-wing, faster, and nicknamed "widow makers" by the flight instructors.

File photograph of a North American SNJ-5 Texan

At Whiting Field near Pensacola, our flight instructors called these "Widow Makers." I had a flight planned to take serial number #13 on Friday the 13th, with training flight number 13. Three different flight instructors asked if I felt ok. I wasn't afraid; I took the flight and passed with an up check.

We were in Ground School one half day and flying one half day. There was a group of cadets from England blended in with us. Because of the English cadets, we were blessed with tea. Tea at breakfast, tea at dinner, tea at supper, but no water. We drank it with sugar, with lemon, and even to this day, I'm still trying to like it. Our ground school became more complicated with Calculus, Morse Code, Celestial Navigation. My roommate was Anderson. His group of Marine fighter pilots had been flying Corsairs at Guadalcanal, who then rotated back to our VRF-2 Squadron. Maxie and his roommate were down the hallway in the same barracks.

Every evening after chow was study time. I think it was intentional that they kept us loaded down. I had never heard of Calculus before, so it was new to me, and Celestial Navigation was challenging and lengthy, because one small error in three pages of multiplying, adding, subtraction would give the wrong answer. Each night just before Taps, Maxie and I would cross check our final answer. We learned that when we got the same answer, we had to be correct. One day, the lieutenant instructor put his answer to the assigned problem on the blackboard; it differed from mine and Maxie's. My confidence was nearly shattered. In my mind, I thought I must have made a mistake.

Then Maxie did the impossible and suggested to the instructor that the answer on the blackboard was in error.

Other cadets in other classes who made that type of suggestion to our instructor before got busted out! Our lieutenant became very red faced, but maintained his composure by telling Maxie to prove it. Maxie went to the blackboard and wrote out the first steps, turned and asked me to come up to speed up the process. Fifteen minutes later, we completed our assignment with the same correct answer. The surprise was the lieutenant thanked us and smiled. We were correct.

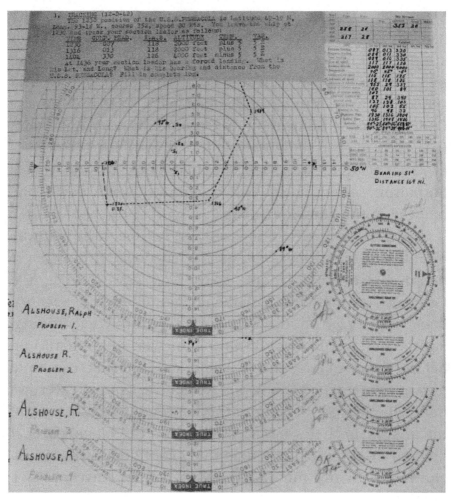

Ensign Alshouse's Celestial Navigation workbook

We learned to fly on instruments in the SNJs. It was our first experience with radios. The downside was one of our cadets crashed into a bulldozer, his plane caught on fire and trapped him screaming in his open mike. It made all of us shudder and to be more careful. Our crash death rate seemed high, but pilots were needed as quickly as possible for the fleet.

Upon completion of Whiting Field training (I never saw Maxie again) 10 of us were sent to Main Station for Scout Observation flight training in OS2Us used aboard battleships and cruisers. Only five of us completed this final phase and received our Navy Wings of Gold!

Storm in the Gulf

One of the planned training sequences at our single engine scout observation squadron was a night navigation flight. Three cadets were each assigned an OS2U airplane. We were briefed to fly 40 minutes in a south-southeasterly direction, make a right turn of 105 degrees, proceed for 35 minutes, make another right turn and come back to base.

File photograph of a Voight OS2U-3

A sturdy but underpowered airplane. I got to "meet" the Admiral of Pensacola Naval Air Station twice flying OS2Us. Completed flight training early; ten cadets started, five completed the program. My reward was to spend days "towing" targets—only got shot up once! The OX-1 was replaced by the OS2U.

Cadets Nessen, Poole, and I climbed into our three planes after dark, started the engines, and taxied out to the assigned take-off area. Our radios were all in good working condition. Cadets Nessen and Poole decided I should take off first, and they would fly loose-wing on me.

Once in the air, we joined up and circled our squadron base. I radioed our altitude, course heading, and time of departure.

Night flying is great! The visibility at night was clear, the air was still, and the stars sparkled brightly. The planes' engines were running perfectly. We each reviewed our navigation on our individual plotting boards that pulled out from under the instrument panel to a position above the knees and the control stick.

We chatted briefly about our compass headings and directional gyros. I noticed my directional gyro was drifting from its original heading. Twenty minutes passed into our assigned flight when we noticed lightning ahead. In another five minutes, we could see the storm. It was a line front.

I radioed the other two cadets about turning before we flew into the storm. They each replied that we were under orders to fly for 40 minutes on this course.

I radioed back to our squadron base for permission to turn on 35 minutes. Our base replied, but there was too much static from the lightning to understand what they said. I remembered our aerology instructor stating, "Never fly into a storm." I radioed Cadets Nessen and Poole that I was changing course. They elected to stay on the original course.

This was my first storm at sea. The whites, reds, blues and even some green colors were so much brighter than any I had seen before.

I made my right turn, proceeding to Point B. I then turned right again and headed back to base. This turn took me away from the storm front and reduced the radio static. I radioed the other two planes, but received no reply.

I checked my plotting board, scanned the instruments and noted my directional gyro seemed to drift even more. Minutes upon minutes passed with a growing, empty feeling of being alone in the night. My OS2U engine was running very smoothly as I switched fuel tanks. I was now on the last main gas tank as both wing tanks were empty.

The minutes wore on and on. I kept checking my instruments and indicators over and over. I thought I should arrive at base soon, but all I could see was blackness. Had I made a fatal mistake? Where were Cadets Nessen and Poole? I hoped they were coming in behind me. The stars lost their sparkle, the darkness seemed blacker. Was I lost?

I saw a faint flicker of light ahead, then another as the base beacon light came into view. It looked so beautiful in the distance. I made a 360-degree circle looking back for my two friends. I radioed them, received no reply and headed for home base. One mile out, I radioed for landing instructions. I was cleared to land with no other planes in the traffic pattern.

After landing in the water beside four lighted buoys, I taxied to our squadron area. Our steam crane operator lifted my plane out of the water and placed the frame on the dolly wheels again. I climbed out and walked to the pilot's ready room, watching for my two friends in the distant darkness.

I reported to the squadron commanding officer. He had received our message requesting a change of course, and had granted permission. I told him about the line front storm in the Gulf. He said it was impossible as they had no other reports of such a storm.

"Sir, there is a storm out there. I changed course early. Cadets Nessen and Poole felt they were under orders to fly 40 minutes on our heading. The pattern took them into the line front storm."

"One more thing, Sir," I said. "I am tired and hungry. It has been noon since the three of us have eaten. They are about out of gasoline, wherever they are."

He looked at his watch. He frowned, picked up the phone and called the tower. The tower operator could not see them or hear them on the radio.

I requested a repair report for my plane so I could explain the drifting directional gyro.

Thirty minutes passed. Both the operations officer and I paced the pilot's ready room floor. Finally, he decided they must be down at sea and a search group must be ready to leave at daylight. All seaplanes, 0S2Us and PB2Ys that were airworthy would be in the search. A briefing was set for 0500, with an estimated time for departure at 0620. He said I would fly my same plane in the morning and for me to get some sleep. Then he handed me a candy bar.

Shot at Sunrise

It was 0130. I walked the many blocks back to my room, past the chow hall and the Officer of the Day's (OD) office. These were the only two buildings with all the lights on. I found my room down the dimly lit hallway. My good friend and roommate, Wes, jumped up when I came in. "Where have you been?" he asked. "You had a midnight watch. Look at this note pinned to your bunk."

I explained my night flight to Wes, the two lost friends, and the search planned for the morning. I also told him he would likely be part of the search with the PB2Ys.

I unpinned the note, read it and walked back to the OD's office. I walked in, saluted, and identified myself. For the next six minutes, I stood at attention, focused on a wall clock while he yelled at me. First in one ear, then the other. I could feel his lips on my ear lobes. I still remember the part about being "shot at sunrise" because I missed a watch (an assigned duty). I even thought about my father, with his great combat career in World War I; he would be very disappointed in me, his son.

By 0200, the OD had tired of yelling and asked, "Where have you been?"

"Flying Sir," I replied.

"That's a damn lie," he yelled again.

"Sir, please. Phone VO Squadron Seven and ask them," I requested.

The OD phoned my squadron. His voice started very loudly, then reached a normal tone, and then I heard him whisper something about two missing planes. He hung up the phone, turned to me and said, "Cadet, I'll take you back to your barracks in my Jeep."

I looked at him, smiled and replied, "No thank you, Sir. I'll walk."

We never found the missing airplanes or the pilots.

The Day I Discovered Admirals were Great

My final squadron training at the Pensacola Naval Air Station was in a 0S2U scout observation plane for potential assignment on battleships and cruisers.

One nice, early September morning in 1943, with a 28-knot wind from the north, I was scheduled to complete a series of buoy landing training flights. After completing 10 water landings near an assigned buoy, I returned the 0S2U to our base. Navy rules state that a pilot must report any damage or repair needed to an aircraft he had just flown. With no known damage or repair needed, I reported to the pilot's ready room.

Fifteen minutes passed before I was requested to report to the squadron's commanding officer (CO). He began yelling that I had broken the main struts between the main pontoon and the fuselage of the 0S2U I had just flown. I tried to explain to him I had not made any hard landings, but it was useless. He took me out to the hangar area, and there my airplane sat. Each strut was bent in the middle with a jagged, gaping open break.

I was still trying to explain to the CO that I had not made any hard landings, when the chief mechanic came close to me and said, "Look at the rust in those breaks." I looked closely and sure enough, each one was rusty. Rust does not form on iron that fast, even in salt water. I pointed the rust out to the CO who was talking about a court martial which would end my flying.

One more time, I told our CO that I had not made any hard landings. He asked, "Can you prove that? Was anyone watching?" I told him that an older gray-haired civilian had been fishing near here and he might have been watching. The CO directed, "Go get him."

I ran in that direction. As I approached the gray-haired man, he was reeling in his line. I introduced myself and explained I had been flying an 0S2U making practice buoy landings. I asked him if he had seen me make any hard landings. He said I had not, and he had been watching closely because the water was so rough.

I explained about the bent struts and the rust. I asked him if he would be so kind as to tell my CO that I had not made any hard landings. He said he would, handing me his bait bucket.

All eyes were upon us as we approached the hangar area where the damaged 0S2U sat. My new acquaintance nodded to the group of officers, then he looked closely at the broken struts. He turned and beckoned me to come over to him. As we walked directly to the CO and a group of other officers, I noticed they were standing at attention. Facing my CO, we stopped. The fisherman put his hand on my right shoulder and said, "This cadet did not make any hard landings this morning. It takes hours for rust to form on iron, even in salt water. That damage had to be from a previous flight."

My CO, standing at attention, saluted and said, "Yes Sir, Admiral Grow!"

The words "Admiral Grow" raced through my mind. I turned and looked him in the face. He smiled at me. I became flustered and shook his hand, muttering something of a thank you. He reached over, took his bait bucket, turned and walked off toward his headquarters office.

That was the day I realized Admirals were great!

***

I later learned Rear Admiral Bradford Grow became a Naval Aviator in 1926 and led a squadron of amphibious planes on a historic 1939 round-trip flight between San Diego and Panama without refueling to demonstrate the aircraft's capabilities.

Ensign Nolz and the Battle of Truk

In early October 1943, Cadets Leo Nolz, Paul Ernsberger, Bill Conklin, Tom Douglas and I were in the final stages of flight training with OS2Us. Leo Nolz's girlfriend and her parents were traveling to Pensacola Naval Air Station, so they could get married just as soon as we got our Navy Wings of Gold. A problem developed with Leo getting a down check in one of his training flights. Leo became so nervous that we questioned his ability to pass his next check flight. Our little group had a quick meeting and decided that I should put on Nolz's flight gear and take his flight for him. We were under immense pressure every day in flight training. I didn't think it was fair to bust a good pilot who simply had a bad day and I had been able to get an up check for Nolz. It was something we did, looking out for each other.

Ensigns Nolz, Conklin, Ernsberger, Douglas and I received our Wings and orders, October 26, 1943. Nolz, Ernsberger and Conklin had orders to go to a flight facility in Ohio. I had orders to go aboard the USS Colorado in the Pacific. Nolz became extremely serious, insisting that he trade orders with me. We went back into the building, and Nolz asked Navy personnel to trade our orders. They gladly accepted his request.

At the time, I was ambivalent about trading orders with Nolz. In my mind, whether I went now or later, I had an unshakable belief I would eventually receive orders to serve in the Pacific.

Ensign Nolz was married early that evening. He had a few days leave and then traveled to the battleship USS Colorado. Nolz and I corresponded for several months. I received a letter from Nolz written the evening of February 17, 1944. Nolz had helped sink two Japanese battleships by correcting the range for the big guns on battleships and cruisers.

Scout planes flew near the targets and would radio back the correct range to hit the target. No one told us we would be the first to be shot down. Without eyes, few targets could be hit. This was before radar. Ensign Nolz landed on the water with his OS2U two times to pick up seven F6F pilots shot down that day. His propeller had to be replaced because of chopping all that water spray.

File photograph of a Vought O2U-2

The Battle of Truk, code named Operation *Hailstone*, took place on February 17 and 18. Ten major Japanese ships were sunk, and 56 were damaged. Five American aircraft carriers were in the task force, carrying 72 F6F fighter planes. At 0443 on the 17th, the first F6Fs were launched. They were able to catch 365 Japanese aircraft on the ground. Two hundred sixty-six of them were destroyed or damaged.

At 1815, the Japanese attacked the task force with their remaining 90 aircraft. The 72 F6F Navy fighter planes on the carriers had time to refuel and rearm to meet this attack. It is estimated that 76 Japanese planes were shot down, and the remaining ones were so damaged that they retreated to their base airport. Seven F6F fighters were shot down.

The strike on Truk in the South Pacific demonstrated a virtual revolution in Naval warfare. The aircraft carrier emerged as the capital ship of the future for the U.S. Navy. The Battle of Truk was also Pearl Harbor in reverse, with no more or less damage to the enemy than what we had suffered at Pearl Harbor.

I learned that Lt. Nolz was shot down on April 20, 1945, during the Battle of Okinawa. He proved his mettle as a combat pilot, and earned his wings every day he was in the South Pacific.

***

Even if we had thought about it, we were too distracted and busy to capture all the experiences happening to us. We knew if we succeeded in flight training, we would fly some of the Navy's newest aircraft, most of which we knew nothing about. I came upon this description of flight training from another Navy pilot assigned to ferry aircraft for the war effort.

MY INTRODUCTION TO THE HELLCAT

By Naval Aviator Norbert Aubuchon

I was trained to fly off a cruiser or battleship as an observation pilot scouting for the enemy or observing and reporting on the shots fired by the ship's big guns. Such duty involved a relatively light, low-powered, single-engine seaplane which was launched by catapult from the ship as it cruised the open sea in search of the enemy. The final training for this duty at Pensacola included three frightening catapult shots off an old dock and into the bay in a Vought O2U-2 on floats. After that, I was 23-years-old, a designated Naval Aviator, with the right to wear the coveted WINGS OF GOLD.

At this point, my navigation training qualified me only for flying over water. So, instead of being assigned to a cruiser or a battleship, the Navy changed its mind and sent me and five other budding ensigns to the Naval Air Station New York, aka, Floyd Bennett Field. We were to help test and ferry the thousands of new combat aircraft pouring out of seven aircraft plants between Baltimore, MD and Stratford, CT. All our flying from then on would be done over land in much larger and, by comparison, frightfully high-powered, and much larger aircraft.

Even though the Navy people at Floyd Bennett were under great pressure to move aircraft, they took pains to train us in cross-country navigation—something entirely new to us seaplane pilots. We were used to flying two-seat training aircraft; the second seat for the instructor whose goal was to keep you from killing yourself.

The catch was that the planes we were to test and ferry were fleet type, single-seat fighters and bombers. Even for experienced pilots, the new powerful war birds were intimidating. For the novices like me, a fresh, untried graduate from flight school at Pensacola, these machines were more than intimidating. The idea of flying an airplane with four times the power of anything we had flown before and doing so without the benefit of an instructor was more than bone-chilling scary. It was terrifying and a clear-cut threat to my underwear.

But there was no other way to learn to fly these machines. These were single-seat airplanes-no room for an instructor. Take my first flight in the Grumman Hellcat fighter for example. The reality of a 2,200-horsepower engine turned out to be power beyond my comprehension. I was given a skimpy how-to-fly-the-Hellcat book published by the manufacturer. And I got a cockpit checkout by a pilot who had flown the type at least once. His lecture comprised of a brief introduction to a maze of fifteen or twenty instruments and the location of a dozen or so essential controls like the throttle, fuel mixture, fuel pump, propeller control, landing gear, flaps, tail-wheel lock, tail hook, emergency procedures, and how to start the engine.

Finally, after wishing me good luck, he warned me that the rate of acceleration of the Hellcat was considerable. He also warned that should there be a plane taking off ahead of me, I should not start until I was sure that plane was in the air. And, so it was. When I was cleared for takeoff, another plane was about half the way down the runway taking off. So, following his advice, when I was sure the plane was in the air, I applied full throttle. The noise was beyond imagination, my body was pressed hard against the seat and the machine seemed to jump into the air. Despite the precaution, I was overtaking the plane ahead at a dangerous rate.

To avoid a midair collision, I banked to the right and the plane disappeared under my left wing. To see where it was, I poked my head out of the cockpit and slightly into the air stream. As I did, the wind suddenly ripped off my sunglasses, snatched my map out of my hand, and yanked my earphones off my head and out into the slipstream—all in one split second. Finally, as the disorienting experience simmered down, alternated glances ahead and at the instrument panel told me I was approaching New York City at a dangerously low altitude at an unbelievable 275 miles an hour. This was a record-breaking speed for me. By this time, I had been in the air all of about three minutes wondering why I had not joined the infantry.

The Day I Sank a Submarine

Another planned training sequence in the Scout Observation Squadron was dive bombing. The OS2U airplanes were not designed as dive bombers, but they could be used as a dive bomber when necessary after a German U-boat or two had sunk several ships in the Gulf of Mexico.

Dive bomb training was accomplished using smoke bombs. With good training and practice, we could drop a smoke bomb in a two-foot square target. Some of us had dive bombing practice in the morning and then towed sleeve targets in the afternoon.

All the flying must have worn out my listening ability. Thursday's briefing was on the art of dropping depth charges. The procedure was the same as dive-bombing, but the depth charges were supposed to be 10-12 feet to the side of the vessel. Following the briefing, seven of us cadets were assigned planes, and our instructor was in the eighth OS2U, as commander of the flight.

Once in the air, we joined formation with the instructor, and he led us toward the target area. On approach, we could see a well-equipped barge-like vessel towing a small target submarine on long cables. Circling our target, the instructor ordered me to dive first.

I went into the dive and zeroed in dead center on the target submarine, pulled the bomb release lever, and pulled up out of the dive. I was joining the rest of flight group when our instructor began telling me over the radio about what a dumb pilot I was. He said something about my sinking the submarine target, and that it would cost the Navy a bunch of money to get it repaired.

We all returned to base.

Climbing out of our planes, the instructor took me to the squadron commanding officer (CO). I thought, "Here we go again, this is really serious this time."

The CO listened to the instructor relating how I had sunk the target submarine. He turned to me and said, "Cadet, you are going to the admiral right now. He will set the discipline."

I was escorted to the admiral's office and was told that he was expecting me. I knocked, entered, saluted and identified myself. Expecting the worst, I was surprised when Admiral Bates stood up, walked around his desk and shook my hand.

He said, "Many flight instructors have tried to sink that target submarine, but only dented it."

I returned to our OS2U training squadron. My first—and only—submarine!

File photograph of an OS2U Kingfisher

Ten Naval Aviators were assigned to single engine seaplane training.

Leo Nolz

Paul Ernsberger

Tom Douglas

Bill Conklin

Ralph Alshouse

All five of this close-knit group received their Navy Wings of Gold 10-26-43.

VRF-2

Aircraft Ferry Squadron 2

In January 1942, the Marines had twelve pilots who had just completed gunnery training at Fort Lauderdale, FL. Their airplanes were F4F fighters; the pilot had to crank the landing gear up or down manually. The aircraft carrier was at San Diego, CA.

These twelve pilots were to fly their planes to the carrier. A problem developed because only six arrived. Five got lost and crashed; one was never found. The admirals concluded that there was only one group of pilots that could fly from point A to point B without getting lost. They were called Barn Stormers, those who gave airplane rides at state fairs. These pilots did not make much money, but they enjoyed flying.

The Navy called them in, gave them a little training, gave them Gold Navy Wings and commissions. Twenty of them were sent to Floyd Bennett Field east of New York City to form VRF-1. Eight were sent to Columbus, Ohio to a facility called Port Columbus.

File photograph of a Curtiss SB2C Helldiver

I had many hours in these. My most memorable flight in the SB2C was when a nurse was hitching a ride in the back seat. She had loosened her lap belt after I told her to keep it on and tight. When I rolled the aircraft, the nurse wound up plastered in the canopy.

The SB2C Wright-Cyclone engine had issues with failing magnetos—engineers found out it was because of a build-up of static electricity on the aircraft and the installation of static wicks solved the high failure magneto rate.

In October 1943, four of us new pilots from Pensacola, FL were sent to Ohio. Upon arrival, each of us were assigned a barnstormer as a flight leader, and we were his wingmen. Charlie Greer was my flight leader. We were assigned a new SB2C dive bomber and to fly them to a big Naval Air Station in San Diego, CA, then hurry back so we could deliver many more airplanes. Plus, we were given new wrist watches, a government check book, a new parachute, a priority card, several airway maps (roads in the sky), a .38 caliber handgun, and a room in the new Bachelor Officer Quarters (BOQ). Plus, a heavy sheep-skin lined jacket with sheep-skin pants that had zippers on each leg, then a warm helmet with two ear cups built in so we could hear. It was made clear that these were for us to use, and we were to return them to the flight equipment quartermaster when the war was over.

Ensign Alshouse in heavy sheepskin-lined flying coveralls

In December 1943, more "green" pilots arrived and VRF-2 Squadron was formed. Johnny Rembert was our first skipper. Johnny was a good manager and was promoted several times. The last time I saw him and talked briefly with him, he was an Admiral. He was replaced as our VRF-2 skipper with Whiskey Pete Peterson.

Commander Peterson did not allow us to much time for leisure for when we were not delivering airplanes, we got checked out in several different aircraft to improve our airmanship and aircraft knowledge.

The Aircraft of VRF-2

Aircraft I flew only once or very rarely included the Cessna T-50.

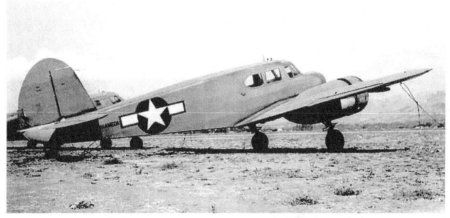

File photograph of a Cessna T-50

We delivered SB2Cs to Norfolk, VA three times, and the squadron T-50 picked us up for the return trip to Columbus, Ohio. On one occasion, as we approached Ohio, one engine failed, causing us to put on parachutes, but we landed safely on one engine.

File photograph of a Howard NH-1

The Operations Officer liked this airplane so much it became his "personal" aircraft. It was an honor if he let you fly "his" airplane.

File photograph of an N2S Stearman

File photograph of an N3N-3

We also trained in these in Minnesota.

File photograph of an OX-5 Swallow

Just checked out in this airplane.

File photograph of a Navy RAD

The Operations Officer had us checked out in the RAD; I never delivered one.

File photograph of a Douglas SBD

The Operations Officer had us checked out in the SBD; if we were called to fly them, it wouldn't be a surprise. It was a good airplane. They were used in the Battle of Midway.

My Most Embarrassing Moment

After flight school and before reporting to duty at Port Columbus, I received a short leave. I went home to Iowa for a few days where Dad took me to a local American Legion meeting to show off his son, the pilot, complete with Wings of Gold.

Ensign Ralph Alshouse

It was a difficult trip from Oelwein, IA to Columbus, Ohio. All day, all night. My flight school classmate, Paul Ernsberger, met me at the train station. Paul had received his wings the same time I received my wings. Paul lived near Port Columbus. Our first few weeks in the squadron were spent being checked out in different airplanes to improve our flight experience.

The second week in December, I was assigned my first, and only flight leader, Charley Greer. A wonderful leader and a religious Quaker, Charley said he requested me to be his wing man. Our first flight together as lead and wingman, we took new SB2Cs to the west coast. We made shorter flights so Charley could teach me the aircraft's refueling system. One of the stops was at Abilene, TX, then to San Pedro Naval Base in California, where we delivered our planes. We returned to Port Columbus on the airlines using our government-issued check books. Our next flight was to Norfolk, VA where Charley decided I should make all the radio calls while he picked the airports for us to refuel on our way to San Diego, CA. We were delayed because of bad weather several times; he never took chances with the aircraft we were to deliver or my education as a pilot. The next two delivery assignments, Charley had me leading the flight and making the radio calls. He just flew wing on me, making sure I made no mistakes. That is how, on the recommendation of Charley, I was checked out to fly cross-country all by myself. All of my flight training had come down to this moment. I was delivering war birds, solo.

In April 1944, I took a new SB2C to San Pedro, CA. For some reason, I took my white uniform with me. Because of bad weather, I stopped at Abilene, TX for the night. My motel room was near this restaurant that Charley liked. I put on my white uniform, I walked in and was seated in a booth. I ordered a T-bone. The place was almost full of Army officers and their wives or girlfriends. I could almost feel being watched as the only Navy officer in the room. When my steak arrived, it was extremely tough, and while trying to carve a nice piece to eat, the whole steak slipped off the plate and fell into my lap. The roar of laughter in the restaurant was instantaneous. I was so embarrassed! I turned a dozen shades of red. With my uniform ruined, I finished that steak and never returned to that restaurant.

I Should Have Said, "Yes."

In early 1944, after delivering an aircraft to the Port of Los Angeles, I was taken to a hangar in the Los Angeles area by Engineer Roy Roepke. In the hangar sat this beautiful, yellow flying wing airplane. Northrop's Flying Wing.

Having not seen one before, I walked around it (no tail) with pusher motors. Mr. Roepke said they were looking for a test pilot to fly it. It had not been off the ground—yet. I said, "NO!"

Months later, I had a few regrets. I should have said, "YES" to test and fly the new design.

Forced Landing at the Gaba Ranch

Sometimes you can meet the nicest people following a forced landing. Hart and Connie Gaba are good examples of nice people. They lived fifty miles east of Alamogordo, NM. Their ranch was 51,000 acres and the nearest telephone was in Alamogordo.

I was west bound with a TD2C. I had refueled at Midland, TX, cleared for El Paso, noting it had been closed earlier that morning. El Paso was open for two reports. I knew the Guadalupe Mountains were an easy landmark and so was the Rio Grande River.

File photograph of a Culver TD2C

We had more fun with these bright red airplanes. They were very hot little airplanes with superb performance and nimble in the air.

The TD2C stalled at 95-98 mph.

I was flying tight wing in one on one of my friends just north of the Texas border. During tight wing, you watch nothing else but your lead. He had led me into a tornado spout at about 5-to-6,000 feet above the ground. The tornado threw me out of sideways, upside down, in an unusual attitude. I recovered about 1,000 feet above the ground. I was rattled, but there was no damage to the TD2C.

I departed from Midland about 1230 p.m. and headed for El Paso with a compass heading of 260 degrees. I flew around several cumulonimbus rainstorms maintaining VFR flight conditions.

Somehow, the Guadalupe Mountains never came into view, and the ceiling was lowering. I entered a wide valley. In a few minutes the valley had a huge, billowing cloud across it. I changed directions heading south-southwest intending to intercept the Rio Grande River.

Soon the only open route was another wide valley that had a cloud ceiling lower than the mountain tops on each side. This lasted a few minutes, then both ends closed.

I began looking for a place to land. It was lightly raining when I found a straight, narrow road made by a bulldozer's blade clearing brush and cactus. A ranch house was about a mile away, so I buzzed it, hoping to get their attention in case I crashed.

I landed on a narrow, sandy-like soil road. My wings cut the brush on both sides. After shutting off my engine, I could see in the distance a very dark horse and rider heading for the ranch house and corrals. Soon a pickup truck came in my direction from the ranch house area.

Hart Gaba and his ten-year-old son arrived and introduced themselves. The son marveled at the airplane, so I invited him to sit in it.

I asked, "What part of Texas are we in?"

Hart laughed and laughed.

"We are in New Mexico," he said.

I asked to use their telephone to call the El Paso airport to tell them where I was. Hart looked at his son and smiled before turning to me to say, "The nearest phone is fifty miles away in Alamogordo."

While we visited, the Gaba family explained that this was the time for the annual fall roundup. They had spent the past several weeks sorting, cutting back, and grouping cattle to sell. The area ranchers had gotten together earlier to decide when each rancher would have their cattle in Alamogordo and on which day. Hart's date was three days away, and it took two days to drive them in.

They were very short-handed, and all three Gabas drove cattle and rode their own horses. Hart asked me to stay and help, saying he would furnish the horse and saddle. I was still thinking when he offered his horse and saddle. I did not know until years later that a rancher cannot offer more. This honor was greater than money.

I thanked Hart for his offer, but felt my job was to the war effort.

Driving me to Alamogordo, Hart mentioned a pickup truck lasted two or three years. The rocks, ruts and washouts that we drove over convinced me. We arrived in town, and he let me off at a phone while he went to the post office.

Our Navy liaison officer in El Paso said he would try to fly out in a light airplane that same afternoon or the next morning. He agreed to report to our VRF-2 squadron I would RON (Remain Over Night).

Hart came back, and we drove to the grocery store. On the way back to the ranch, I listened to a lengthy history of the ranch. He said that in the last few years he had built the ponds, a small irrigation system for hay production, and the primitive "roads" on the ranch.

As we approached the ranch house, Hart mentioned he needed to repair a water gap fence. He invited me to accompany him. We spliced wire, set posts, stretched and attached barbed wire across a dry creek bed.

We heard a light plane in the distance and drove from our completed fence repair towards my TD2C, about two miles away. Arriving at my plane, the search plane spotted us. They flew down, rocked the wings and headed towards El Paso. It was getting late, only thirty minutes until sunset. We decided they would be back in the morning.

Returning to the ranch house, Hart explained to Connie that I would be staying overnight. She suggested he milk the cows before it got too dark while she fixed supper.

Hart picked up two milk buckets and headed for the corrals with me following. After walking through three gates, he sat one pail down and walked over to a Holstein-Guernsey cow. He patted her, squatted down beside her and started milking.

I looked at the other two cows. One appeared to be dry, so I picked up the other milk pail and walked over to a Jersey-Guernsey cow. I patted her, squatted down and started milking her.

"Hey!" Hart hollered in surprise.

I looked over at him and asked, "Don't you want this cow milked?"

Yes." He replied. "I thought you were a city kid."

At supper Hart teasingly said I should have landed about ten miles south. I asked why, and Connie interrupted to describe their local school teacher and the one-room schoolhouse. Hart agreed with her with a nod and a wink.

Breakfast the next morning of eggs, potatoes and steak at this New Mexico ranch tasted much better to me than at the best restaurant in New York City. We were finishing a cup of coffee when we heard the sound of a light plane.

All four of us drove out to where my TD2C plane waited.

Our Navy liaison officer landed near my plane. He was glad to see my TD2C was undamaged. He explained it would take three to four days to get a truck in to haul my plane back to the El Paso airport. He asked if I thought I could fly it out of the wide canyon.

With everyone looking at me, I said that I thought I could if we could reduce the aircraft's weight and thin out the number of the rocks on the eight-foot-wide roadway.

The Gaba family worked on the rock problem while the liaison officer and I removed the non-working radio, took my small bag, my zipper case of maps and my parachute to his plane. We also drained some of the gasoline from my plane's tank.

Everything was ready. I climbed into my TD2C and started the engine. With help on each wing tip, we got the plane turned around. I taxied past the turn in the narrow road to get all the speed I could on the straight-away. Everyone again helped on the wing tips to get the plane turned into the light wind.

With a thumbs up gesture, I opened the throttle of my 120-horsepower engine, made the turn in the road, and headed down the stretch.

It seemed like my plane would never lift off, and the straight away was ending. In a desperate gamble, I pulled back on the stick, flipped the landing gear switch to retract it and prayed. I was cutting brush with my propeller.

I heard the landing gear clank as it completed its retraction. I was still flying.

Now I could gain enough altitude to get my propeller out of the brush. I thought I was climbing adequately until I glanced ahead to see a big Saguaro cactus on an upward slope, with its arms spread wide. There was no way I could get over it at the altitude I was at.

I dipped my left wing into the brush tops, pushed a little on my left rudder to just slide by Mr. Saguaro Cactus.

I remained at the low-level, but now I could get up to cruising speed. When I did, I turned 180 degrees, buzzed my friends on the ground, and headed for the El Paso airport.

Automatic Pilot at the Wrong Time

The OS2U Kingfisher was a very reliable scout observation plane. It was being replaced by the SC-1 which was a faster plane with more horsepower. Another feature of the SC-1 was an automatic pilot.

Scout observation planes aboard battleships and cruisers were the eyes of the big ships. No one ever explained it, but it made sense that in war, both sides tried very hard to eliminate the enemy's eyes. I was assigned to take a new SC-1 from Port Columbus to San Diego, CA. This machine had a fixed landing gear until it got near its ship, then pontoons were installed.

My SC-1 had short-range requiring many refueling stops. Arriving in Abilene, TX for more gas, I filed a flight plan for El Paso, TX. With the control tower's permission, I taxied out near the active runway. Running up the engine, I checked both magnetos and found them to be okay. I radioed the control tower, asking for permission to take off.

With no other planes in the traffic pattern, the tower cleared me for takeoff. I pulled the plane onto the runway, positioned it and opened the throttle. My SC-1 responded well on take-off. Climbing up and out, away from the airport, I had only reached 200 feet above ground level (AGL) when the controls set up. The plane was trying to turn to the right. I found I could muscle control it.

The tower asked if I was in trouble. I grabbed the microphone to say, yes, I was in trouble and I would try to make it back to the field. The airport rolled out the emergency equipment.

Using both hands on the stick, I made a 180-degree turn at 200 feet AGL. The wind velocity was only 5 mph, so I elected to make a downwind landing. My only downwind landing.

I landed safely and met the fire trucks and ambulances heading out. They had not expected me to land downwind.

The mechanics found that the automatic pilot had come on even though the on-off switch was pointing to off. They disconnected the automatic pilot, allowing me to continue on my way to San Diego.

File photograph of a Curtiss SC-1 like the one I experienced an unintended activation of the automatic pilot. It seemed I was the only one in the squadron who flew these. It replaced the OS2U.

Closed to Instrument Landings

One of the least intelligent episodes two experienced Navy pilots ever had was landing two airplanes at an airport closed to instrument landings.

Lt. Bud Penniman and I were taking our assigned TD2Cs to Santa Ana, CA. We had gotten to our last refueling stop at El Centro, CA about noon. Checking the weather, we found the coast was fogged in until 0900. This was normal. The next three weather reports were VFR, Visual Flight Rules, four miles and a 1,500-foot ceiling.

Bud and I cleared VFR for Santa Ana. Our fast, little TD2Cs had retractable landing gear, a fuel gauge, compass, a needle ball instrument, tachometer and a simple altimeter. Our TD2Cs did have radios, but neither one of them worked.

File photograph of Naval Air Station Santa Ana

Getting up over the Vallecito Mountains was routine. We could see the overcast extending west. It appeared to end about 10-15 miles away, so we flew west expecting to descend along the Pacific coastline.

All TD2C pilots know their airplane has only a two-hour fuel-range. By the time Bud and I had flown to the edge of the overcast, an hour and fifteen minutes had passed. The edge of the overcast was only the edge of the upper layer of clouds. Several hundred feet lower, it was still overcast. Through hand and arm signals, Bud insisted he fly wing on me. This is where instrument ratings and experience are useful, even when we lacked the instruments and equipment, like a working radio.

We let down at five hundred feet per minute heading 270 degrees. I was praying the ceiling was seven to eight hundred feet. I am sure Bud was praying too. Bud was flying tight wing position. I watched my altimeter unwind. Twelve hundred feet, nine hundred feet, six hundred feet, three hundred feet. Now we had a serious problem! Would we see the water before we flew into it? I reduced our rate of descent to two hundred feet per minute. Now we were at two hundred feet, one hundred feet, seventy-five feet, fifty feet. We broke through at forty feet. I glanced at Bud. He wanted the lead so I flew wing on him.

Bud was from California. He knew California's weather. At least he must have had a plan. We flew along the coast, just out over the water because the ceiling was so low. He had his map out looking intently. I thought we could land on the beach or any airport we came to if it came to that. Our gas gauges were getting low. The ceiling was still at forty feet and the visibility was a mile, give or take.

The next few minutes the visibility degraded to less than five hundred feet. We were flying at 125 miles per hour. We reached the Santa Ana airport because the railroad ran their tracks right beside the airport.

Santa Ana was also a blimp base. We had been warned to not fly under a blimp when they are moored because ropes and cables secure them. Bud weaved his way through and around four blimps, did a tight 180-degree turn and landed near the tower. I remained right behind him!

We stepped out of our airplanes and I grabbed Bud's hand in respect for him getting us to our destination.

I asked, "How much gas do you have?"

Bud replied, "My gauge reads empty."

"Mine says empty also," I replied.

We walked to the operations office to turn in our log books and close our flight plans.

The operations officer told us the field had been closed for over 45 minutes. He thought we had done very well to land safely.

Bud explained our inability to return to El Centro, and that we had to come to Santa Ana without radios or required instruments.

We never, ever made the mistake of going beyond our point of return again!

Emergency Landing In El Paso

El Paso was the only major airport that had a female control tower operator. She must have been one of the best, but I never had the opportunity to meet her.

I had an SB2C dive bomber going to San Diego. I refueled at Abilene, TX. Flying at 14,000 feet, I was passing over El Paso when my 1,750-horsepower engine died. I switched magnetos, changed fuel tanks, changed prop pitch, swore and prayed. None of these things worked, and I was losing altitude.

I changed my radio receiver frequency to the El Paso tower. I picked up the microphone and called in. I identified myself, gave the tower operator my altitude. I told her I had a dead stick and requested immediate landing instructions saying, "This is an emergency!"

The tower operator gave precise orders to an American Airlines plane that was on final approach to wave off and told all other traffic in the pattern to leave immediately. The plane waiting to be cleared for takeoff was told to return to the parking ramp immediately. The emergency equipment headed for runway 270.

I knew I had only one chance and no mistakes were allowed. I crossed the field positioning myself. Late on the downwind leg, I dropped my landing gear and stayed in close because the SB2Cs glided like a rock, all nine tons of it. I turned on my short final approach and landed. A good three-point Navy landing.

The emergency equipment was just arriving. I did not need them, but it still made me happy.

A tow tractor arrived and attached to my dead SB2C, pulling it off the active runway. Two new magnetos later that day, and I was on my way again.

War Weary SB2C

In late 1944 and early 1945, we found ourselves flying new SB2Cs to the San Diego Naval Air Station so they could go aboard aircraft carriers. We were also flying used, war weary SB2Cs back to Jacksonville, FL for major overhaul. This created a double whammy on one round trip. The new airplanes usually had some bugs in them that came to our attention during the 10-14 hour west-bound flight. The old SB2Cs were so used up that engine failure was common.

File photograph of a Curtiss SB2C-5

My first SB2C flight from San Diego to the Jacksonville rework facility in Florida was exciting! Taking off from San Diego, I headed east up over the mountains. At 13,000 feet, everything seemed to be okay until I noticed the wing folding control handle had worked half-way out. This control is used to fold the aircraft's wings to reduce the aircraft's footprint on the deck of the carriers.

I tried to push it back in with my hands, but failed to get it back into position. I put my right foot on it and pushed. Still no success. All Navy pilots have heard the "instant death" stories when a wing folds in flight. I thought it might be my time. I considered bailing out, but hated to waste an airplane.

I radioed the El Centro tower for landing instructions. It was a nice relief to land safely, taxi in, and push the wing folding control handle back into its "supposed" locked position. This time we safety wired it in closed/locked position.

I refueled and filed a flight plan for Abilene, TX.

I played it safe by leveling off at 15,000 feet Mean Sea Level on this leg of the trip. I flew past Phoenix, then Tucson, with a nice tail wind. My worn-out plane was doing great. Deming Airfield was on the left and in a few minutes, I was passing over El Paso.

Then my engine quit! This time I grabbed the microphone and told the tower operator I had a dead stick and asked her to clear out the traffic. I said I thought I could make it back to the airport and I gave her my altitude and location.

I made it back with plenty of altitude, so I lowered my landing gear a little early. The tower operator asked if I was the same pilot who brought in a dead stick two days ago.

I replied, "Yes. I'll probably need two more new magnetos again."

My landing was a little longer this time. The fire trucks and emergency equipment men were also happy as they turned to head back to their stations.

Rime Ice on the Wings

Early in 1945, I was ordered to take an FG-1 Corsair to the Marines at Fort Lauderdale, FL. They had a fighter group ready to ship out, but needed one more plane. The weather was marginal, but VFR conditions were 1,000 feet and three miles of visibility.

Flying from Port Columbus south over Nashville, TN, I came into light rain. The temperature was slightly above freezing. I pulled on my carburetor heat control. The tachometer increased 200 rpm. That meant I had some carburetor icing. I left the carburetor heat control on to prevent a forced landing from freezing up the carburetor and creating a dead engine.

File photograph of a Goodyear FG-1 Corsair

This was a wonderful aircraft. It had six inches taken off their wing tips, and they were mostly made for the English aircraft carriers. Their aircraft carriers had six-inch lower hangar decks than the U.S. carriers.

I had one catch fire west of Pittsburg, PA. Three of us were headed for Roosevelt Field, NY. I had a flat-out race with a P-51 Mustang and when I used the aircraft's water injection system, I blew past him.

It was probably hard on the new engine, but it was oh so much fun to beat the Mustang!

I began picking up ice on the windshield of the canopy. The older pilots call it rime ice. Rime ice is somewhat like sleet. It attaches to the leading edge of the wings, changes the air flow, and reduces the aerodynamic lift of the wings.

Our ground school instructors had cautioned us and had always advised to change altitude.

The ceiling had improved to 1,300 feet, but that was where I was at. Going higher would be on instrument flying.

I decided to land at Chattanooga, TN airport and quickly called the tower to explain my problems. The tower operator cleared me to land on runway 180. He stated the runway was a little icy. The river was the south boundary of the airport.

In the traffic pattern, I noticed hunks of floating ice in the river at the end of runway 180. I lowered my landing gear, came around on final approach and landed.

The runway was really icy, and I was really busy with the rudder to keep the Corsair moving straight down the runway. I was slowing down but the end of the runway was too close. The airport emergency equipment was approaching the runway.

I was out of landing strip and unable to stop. I opened the throttle, releasing all 2,000 horsepower, pushed the left rudder locking the left brake, pulled the throttle aft, cut the switches, and waited. My big beautiful airplane spun like a top!

I climbed down from the Corsair's cockpit to wait for a tow tractor. The firemen checked the plane and reported no damage, no fire, but lots of ice. They asked why I put the airplane into a spin?

I replied, "I hate swimming in ice water."

Forced Landing in Pittsburgh

A forced landing is a simple choice between life or death. The emphasis is on death and injury. Parachutes are used only when everything else fails.

One of the most beautiful scenes, greatest works of art, the prettiest and most appealing arrangement of material and machines made by man under God's direction, is an airport runway with waiting fire trucks and ambulances. I was bringing in an FG-1 Corsair on fire.

The airport was Pittsburgh's newest and finest. I was told they filmed the entire show. Lt. Ernsberger and Lt Darby and I were delivering three Corsairs to Roosevelt Field for the English (they had English markings on them). The weather was superb as we flew at 7,000 feet altitude.

We had talked about how many snaps rolls a Corsair could do before stalling out. We did not know the answer, so I decided this would be a good time to find out.

All I remember is the Corsair could do a bunch. What I did not know was I had a hydraulic line leaking behind the cockpit. My plane began trailing smoke. Paul Ernsberger and Russ Darby radioed my problem to me. They flew along side of me and indicated they could see smoke, but no flames yet!

We were just west of Pittsburgh and I decided to put it in quick. Paul and Russ agreed to do the radio work just when my radio died. The RT unit (receiver-transmitter) is behind the pilot's seat. I knew whcrc thc fire was.

File photograph of a Goodyear FG-1 Corsair

As I approached the field, they were clearing out all the other traffic. On the downwind leg, I was diving too fast. I dropped the landing gear early and just a little flap. I could smell the smoke and thought I could feel the heat on the back of my seat. Turning on the crosswind leg, I could see fire trucks and ambulances getting in place along both sides of the runway.

My final approach was short, very short. I picked up my left wing and landed full stall on the end of the runway.

The first fire truck started spraying me, but I rolled past. The second fire truck, running on the side of the runway, sprayed me; but I rolled past him too. The third fire truck picked my plane up and stayed on, spraying foam.

Stopping, I unbuckled my seat belt, shoulder harness and parachute and climbed out quickly. I ran from the Corsair.

As I ran towards the spraying fire truck, a fireman wearing an asbestos suit and carrying a fire extinguisher, started running towards my burning plane.

Now those people have guts! They had been well trained and they saved my Corsair.

Five Gallons at a Time

Another Corsair was needed at the Naval Air Station Fort Lauderdale for the Marine contingent assigned there. I arrived about 1100 with the big beautiful new airplane. I loved the Corsair; the long nose, the bent wings, the incredible power. While closing my flight plan and turning in the Corsair's log books, I was asked if I had ever flown a Piper Cub aircraft. I replied yes, but that it had been about three years ago.

The Marine fighter wing had a small cub ambulance plane that needed to go to Memphis, TN for a major overhaul. I was supposed to take it there. The Marine operations officer insisted I take the Cub up and fly around with it a little bit.

I put my parachute, my zipper bag of airway maps and small clothing bag in the Cub. I looked it over and checked the gas and oil.

File photograph of a NE-1 Piper Cub

The four-cylinder engine looked grimy. The airplane was tacky. I climbed in, fastened the seat belt, and signaled the ground crew to pull the prop through with the switch off. I primed the carburetor, called "switch on." I turned the switch on and signaled for a manual prop pull.

The engine started but it was limping. The ground crew chief came to the right side of the plane and walked behind the wing strut brace. He said they had used this limping Cub for about two months. I asked where the door was. He said it had fallen off last year and they did not need it in warm Florida. The ambulance stretcher was located directly behind the pilot's seat. The side opening in the fuselage was made longer so the stretcher could be set in and out quickly, allowing it to be strapped down easily.

I signaled the wheel chock to be removed and then taxied to the runway. I received a green light from the tower because the Cub had no radio. After checking traffic, I revved up and took off. The plane climbed slowly to 1,000 feet. I then left the traffic pattern. I did a power-on stall, then a power-off stall to get the feel of this little machine. I re-entered the traffic pattern at 1,000 feet and received a green light from the control tower. I pulled the throttle back, turned on cross wind, and then turned on final approach.

I was still at 500 feet AGL over the end of the runway. I had forgotten this little machine floats like a glider.

I could see a group of Marine pilots waving and throwing their caps in the air in glee. Embarrassed as I was, I looked around the traffic pattern and saw no other planes were around. I did a 360-degree descending turn and landed on the runway. I taxied up for refueling and received the Marines' teasing as I filed a flight plan for Tampa, FL.

The shortest distance to Tampa is a straight line across the Everglade swamps. My little limping Cub airplane and I were doing fine observing the swamp at about 700 feet altitude. The first hour passed, then the weather clouded up, and I could see spotty rain showers. I easily flew around them at 500 feet AGL.

My fuel gauge was a cork bobber on a kinky wire. It was part of the gas cap located in front of the windshield, so I could not rely on the accuracy of the gauge. According to my wrist watch, I didn't have enough time to fly back through the Everglades.

To my surprise, I spotted three tornado water funnels. They seemed to be about 30 feet wide and 1,500 feet tall. Of the three tornado water funnels, the one on the right appeared to be a farther distance than the other two. I flew low trying to go between them. They were about a mile apart. The turbulence increased and my little airplane turned into a bucking bronco. I noticed the cypress trees were lying almost flat in the wind.

This would have been a terrible place to crash. The alligators would get me before I could be found. I pushed the plane down to near the tree tops. I hoped that there would be less turbulence and less wind velocity at that lower level. The little limping engine never failed. I broke through the squall line and landed in Tampa 20 minutes later.

I quickly refueled and filed a flight plan to Tallahassee. From Tallahassee, I filed a flight plan to Columbus, GA. The head winds must have increased because I ran out of gas. I was forced to do another dead-stick landing in a cow pasture in southern Georgia.

One nice thing about a Cub ambulance airplane is that it can land in almost any decent field most of the time. The cow pasture I found myself in was about 30 acres and it held 16 cows. My trusty little plane sat about ten rods from the road fence. I climbed the fence and stood in the road wondering which way to walk when a Ford pickup appeared.

The driver was a dairy farmer who owned the pasture I had landed in. I told him I needed five gallons of gas so I could proceed to Columbus. He offered to take me to the local gas station and general store about two thirds of a mile down the road.

The store owner had the gas, a five-gallon can and a funnel I could use, but I did not have gas stamps. After several minutes of discussion, I agreed to pay him with a government check (a transportation request).

It was a good feeling to send a RON message to VRF-2. The communication allows the squadron operations office to know each pilot's location, and what he's flying.

After putting the gas in the tank, the farmer helped me start the plane and I continued to Columbus. The next morning, the weather was normal for the year with winds from the west-northwest. I inspected the limping airplane on the flight line. Talking to an Army sergeant, I convinced him I needed an Army five-gallon gas can with a flexible spout and some rope. He was correct that it is not within authorization to carry gas cans in military aircraft; but I needed it to get to the next airport. He agreed to have it sitting by my Cub, so I could tie the full gas can behind the seat. I also "borrowed" a pair of wood aircraft chocks.

Everyone knows southern trains are slow, particularly freight trains. I was actually passed by a freight train that morning. My limping Cub was cruising at 65 mph with a 30 to 35 mph headwind.

Flying over an hour, I looked for a field to land in with a windbreak. I landed, taxied behind the windbreak, and poured the five gallons of gas into the tank. I then chocked the left wheel with a pull rope attached under the plane. I started my engine manually, stepped around under the right wing, pulled the chocks out, tossing them in the stretcher with the gas can.

Flying all day and filling the gas can two more times at small grass strip airfields, I made it to Muscle Shoals, AL. The airport was TVA restricted, and they did not want me to stay. With only 30 minutes before sunset, I could not get out.

One gentleman took me to a little motel in town and agreed to pick me up at 0700. Having breakfast, the next morning, at 0600, I spent the next few minutes waiting for my ride. I started scratching. My bed must have had hungry little insects in it.

After checking my flying machine, I filled the gas tank and the five-gallon gas can. The weather was good, locally, so up and away I went. Flying west, I found a heavy fog area. By flying south-southwest, I was able to stay out of it for a while.

After 30 minutes of flying, the fog bank became a massive wall. Looking for a place to land was limited. There were a lot of small patches of fields with tall trees on all sides. The paved highway seemed to be the best choice. Over the telephone line and under a power line, I landed, stopping near a driveway, I cut off my switch. Climbing out, I pushed the tail into the driveway to get my plane partly off the highway. This was at least my second forced landing with this little airplane.

Soon, a pickup truck came down the road and stopped. The driver was a foreman at a local saw mill. I filled him in on my background and what I was doing.

When the fog lifted, I could leave. The foreman helped me pour the five gallons of gas from the can into the plane's gas tank. He helped me start the plane, then he drove half a mile down the road to stop traffic while I took off.

It felt good to arrive in Memphis, TN with my little limping Cub airplane. I accomplished the impromptu mission, turned in the log books, and returned to Port Columbus.

A Blinding Flash of Light

Flying an SB2C across New Mexico is usually routine. My flight plan to California was to refuel in Tucson, AZ, which is west of Deming. I found it necessary to swing south to get around a very large thunderstorm. The turbulence was substantial and continuous when there was a blinding flash of light. I must have been hit by lightning. I opened and closed my eyes repeatedly but I could not see. I held the stick as steady as possible.

My mind raced and I nearly panicked. *Should I bail out?*

Although I was bouncing all over the sky, my SB2C was trimmed for straight-and-level flight, and my heightened senses convinced me I was not in a spin or an unusual attitude. As I struggled to keep the SB2C straight and level, it seemed that a very long time had passed before I could see just a little. I was thankful my sight gradually returned and I could safely fly my airplane.

My radio had died during the lightning strike. Douglas, AZ was the nearest airport and I needed to land very soon.

I circled the field twice and I was beginning to see well enough when they gave me a green light, so I landed.

The mechanics needed to replace several fuses plus one magneto. I sent a RON message to my home base at Port Columbus.

There was an Army flight surgeon who checked my eyes. He said they would be okay, but they would feel like sandpaper for several days. He put in some eye drops and handed me a small bottle to take with me. It wasn't long before I continued on to California with the SB2C.

Out of Fuel

Flying SB2C war-weary planes from San Diego to Jacksonville, FL was always exciting. I was asked to lead two Marine pilots, so the three of us filed a flight plan to El Paso, TX to refuel.

Arriving near El Paso, I asked the tower controller for landing instructions. The control tower said they were having a sandstorm and we were ordered on to Albuquerque, NM. The three of us headed north.

I radioed the Marines telling them we all needed to drain each wing tank empty, then switch tanks. We were very low on 120 octane gas.

Twenty miles out of Albuquerque, I radioed our position. Their wind was from the north. Five miles out, I requested a formation straight in approach. The Albuquerque tower operator said no.

I radioed, "This is an emergency. We do not have enough fuel to circle the field." We were willing to land in loose formation in order to get down.

The Albuquerque tower said they had a B-29 on final approach ten miles out. I said I was sorry, but we were coming straight in. We had to.

We landed without ever getting permission from the tower. Of our three SB2Cs, two planes needed to be towed from the runway to be refueled. The B-29 told the Albuquerque tower he had plenty of gas and went on around until the runway was cleared.

Unexpected

Rod Moore was the VRF-2 Squadron Operations Officer. He was in his late 40s. To me he was a father image type person. I carried a lot of respect for him, even when he assigned me several "junk" flights. Junk flights were the ones that higher rank pilots did not want to be bothered with or were difficult to accomplish. Or dangerous. Rod's office was on the ground floor of our main hangar, on the south side with crank out windows. Rod sat with his back to the windows.

Just outside the windows sat a bright Navy-blue jeep that we "borrowed" from the Army across the field at the big SB2C factory. On that dark and stormy night, four VRF-2 pilots pushed the olive-drab green Army Jeep across the south end of our airport into our Navy repair shop. The next morning, it came out bright blue with two large fire bottles, one crowbar and one axe. Armed with the freshly painted Jeep, Rod wanted it parked just outside of his windows. He felt he could get to a crash quicker than the fire department, which he did several times. As soon as the airport control tower sounded the alarm, Rod was in "his" Jeep. Several lives were saved this way.

We never knew when the blue Jeep would be needed.

P-47 Thunderbolt Fighter

I had just returned from a delivery flight one morning and was walking towards our main hangar when the control tower sounded the siren: An Army P-47 pilot was taking off and was in trouble. His engine was misfiring and leaving a trail of smoke.

Rod Moore, our Operations Officer, was in his Jeep driven by Ensign Carl Ackerman. As they came around the corner of the main hangar, Rod yelled to me. "Alshouse! Jump in!" They never stopped, but I jumped in. The P-47 was just above treetop height heading east-southeast.

File photograph of a P-47 Thunderbolt

We rolled up to the main gate as another Navy pilot was walking in. Rod called to him to jump in. We headed after the smoking P-47. The plane was below the treetops now.

Carl had to be the best Jeep driver in the world. He was running it wide open and we were hanging on tightly. We could hear the fire equipment sirens behind us.

A plume of smoke ahead of us indicated where the P-47 Thunderbolt had crashed. We came to the farm where the crash site was. The first gate to the barnyard was made of boards. Rod yelled "Duck!" and we drove right through it. The next gate to the pasture was boards. Rod yelled "Duck!" and we drove right through it. The next gate to the pasture had three barb wires. We drove right through the closed gate doing at least 30 mph.

The crashed plane was right side up, landing gear retracted and the right wing was knocked off. Flames were starting to engulf the cockpit, the engine, and where the wing was torn off.

Rod told me to grab a fire bottle from the Jeep and suppress the flames at the engine and the right side of the cockpit. The unknown pilot was asked to use the other fire bottle on the left wing and cockpit. Carl and Rod worked on the closed cockpit hatch with a crowbar and an axe.

We sprayed the engine and both sides of the cockpit. The heat from the fire was trying to chase us away. As the flames were increasing, they quickly got the hatch off. Carl reached in and released the pilot's seatbelt and shoulder harness. Carl and someone else jerked the P-47 pilot up and out. By this time, the cockpit was totally engulfed in flames and both of the portable fire bottles were empty. We all ran towards the Jeep dragging the pilot.

Then Rod yelled "Hit the deck!" The four of us were lying flat on the ground when the plane blew up.

The first fire truck arrived and opened up with foam. An ambulance pulled up near our Jeep, opened the two back doors and grabbed a stretcher. We gently slid the

Army pilot over onto the stretcher and lifted him into the ambulance. They left for the hospital.

My good friend Paul Ernsberger had also responded to the crash and had driven out to the crash site in his car.

Paul looked at me and shouted, "Ralph, you're burned!"

"Yes, just a little," I replied.

That's when we noticed a farmer standing in semi-shock to the north of us. Paul and I walked over to him. He stuttered something while asking who was going to pay for the damages. We assured him that the military would pay if he would make a list of damages.

Paul insisted to take me to sick bay to get patched up. Arriving at sick bay, Paul dropped me off saying he was going down to the main hangar to check the flight schedules. In less than ten minutes, Paul was back. He said I was scheduled for an SB2C bomber to San Diego. It would be a rush flight, the last one to fill a carrier in port.

Paul said he would take me to the BOQ to get clean, unburned clothes, then down to the main hangar for my flight. I made it to Fort Worth, TX just a little after dark with the SB2C. There were no available rooms because I was so late. I pushed two sofa chairs together and fell asleep. It was just getting to be daylight when I awoke all sore and tired and hungry. Someone had left an apple in the ready room; I looked around to see if it belonged to anyone. I was so hungry that I took it and ate it. I filed a flight plan for El Paso to refuel.

I must have strained every muscle in my body responding to the crash for it took an unbelievable effort on my part to climb into my SB2C, fire it up, and head for El Paso.

Sunrise at El Paso

Arriving in El Paso shortly after sunrise from Fort Worth, TX was a peaceful experience. No other airplanes were in the traffic pattern and none were taking off for distant destinations.

Asking the tower for landing instructions brought immediate permission to land on runway 270. Landing on runway 270 was very smooth that morning. They had finally gotten this old strip repaired. Ten months ago, I had jerked the tail wheel assembly completely off an SB2C-3 when I landed it full stall and unintentionally stuck the tail wheel in one of their larger potholes.

After taxiing up to the service mat, I headed for the operations office to file a flight plan for San Diego, CA. Waiting for me was our local liaison officer. This was a big surprise, because we rarely saw him. As we shook hands, I thanked him for flying out to the Hart Gaba ranch to help me retrieve the TD2C.

He said he needed me to return the favor for his help at the Gaba ranch. I told him I would be glad to help him as we walked to the pilot's ready room. He began to explain that a very high-ranking officer needed transportation, when this Navy man with gold bars and stripes all over the right and left sleeves of his uniform introduced himself. The Admiral stated he needed a ride to the west coast immediately.

I explained we used to carry passengers when we had room, but right now we could not because a few had died when we crashed.

This Admiral then explained, that he was the commander of a group of submarines. They were docked south of San Pedro, CA. The subs had been repaired, restocked, and refueled to leave that afternoon. He was here in El Paso and could not get a plane ticket in time.

I stopped myself from making a remark about maybe he used poor planning. He could see I wanted to get on with my flight and not be bothered with the troubles of an Admiral. The Admiral became very serious as he explained he had had eight days to see his wife and their only child, a 23-year-old daughter. His wife was very ill the day he arrived in El Paso. The second day she died. The funeral was two and a half days later. His daughter died the next day. Her funeral had been the day before. All three of us wiped tears from our eyes.

That is when the Admiral put an arm around me and said, "Son, once in a while we have to break the rules to get the job done."

I thought about that for a minute, how I helped Ensign Nolz get an up check, and then replied, "Grab your bags, sir, and let's go." I filed a flight plan for the San Diego Naval Air Station

Cruising west at 14,000 feet altitude in an SB2C dive bomber was rough and bumpy. I picked up my mic and spoke to the Admiral from the Submarine Corps. I explained while we could make better ground speed at this altitude, it would be a lot smoother on him if we climbed a few thousand feet.

His answer was unforgettable. "Son, you are the captain of this ship. I am only your passenger. I like this altitude best."

Coming over the last mountain range into San Diego is usually like entering a beehive of airplanes.

The landing area at San Diego was one large blacktopped area longer than half a mile and almost round. Usually there are so many airplanes and so much radio traffic it did not pay to ask for landing instructions or permission to land. We would usually follow the traffic flow in a left-hand pattern, find a hole on the crosswind leg, turn on final approach, and land. There would be planes ahead, planes on each side and a bunch coming in behind. Once a plane landed, the pilot needed to keep moving as expeditiously as possible to get out of the way.

It must have been about 1100 hours as we flew past the last mountain range. Just to impress the admiral, I picked up the mic, called the San Diego tower and identified my aircraft number and type of airplane. Putting the mic back in its bracket, I had a big surprise. They answered, "Do you have an Admiral on board?"

My answer was, "Roger, I do."

We were given immediate permission to land.

We made a straight in approach. I lowered my landing gear and a little flap. It's always nice to make a perfect landing with so many people watching. I was instructed to taxi to a waiting twin-engine Beechcraft with its engines running. That plane would take the Admiral immediately to his submarines in San Pedro.

As the Admiral climbed out of the back seat of my SB2C dive bomber he looked up at my cockpit and waved goodbye. As I waited with both feet on the brakes and the engine idling, the Admiral was assisted by several ranking officers into the waiting Beechcraft, and the door closed behind him.

The Beechcraft pilots took off right from there. It was a pretty take off. They headed north for San Pedro.

The tower called me as I sat there in amusement. They directed me to follow the "FOLLOW ME" Jeep that would take me over to the aircraft carrier that was docked northwest of our landing mat area. As I taxied my SB2C behind the Jeep, the tower said my plane would be the next one loaded on the carrier, and the carrier would leave at 1200 hours. I looked at my watch, it was 1140 hours.

Two months later, our operations officer, Rod Moore, sent a note for me to see him. The Admiral had sent a letter of commendation up through the Navy channels. I told Rod I thought that was nice of the Admiral. He agreed.

"By the way," Rod said. "I just noticed the date you did this. Were you allowed to carry passengers then?" I told the long story and the reasons I broke the rules. Rod looked at me and said, "If you don't tell anyone, I won't either."

Big White Bird

Sandhill Cranes migrate north through Kansas and Nebraska each year in February and March. They are beautiful, large white birds with long legs.

In late February 1945, I was asked to take an SB2C-5 from Port Columbus to San Diego. There was a sense of urgency that I needed to hurry my departure because a waiting carrier needed a few more airplanes.

File photograph of a Curtiss SB2C Helldiver

It was rare to fly alone. In fact, it was great not having to "herd" green pilots. Little Rock, AR was having bad weather, so I cleared for Wichita, KS.

Nice clear weather was predicted most of the way, with 10-15 miles of visibility over Missouri and Kansas. Every occupation has a day when everything is just about perfect. My factory-new dive bomber was purring like a kitten with no mechanical "bugs" showing up. It was a great day! Even the grass was showing some green this spring day at 6,000 feet altitude.

To save time, I started my let down over the Missouri River. Leaving my throttle setting on cruising. I could increase my ground speed 15-20 knots.

About 30 miles east of Wichita and about 1,400 feet above the ground, I was tuning my radio to the airport frequency. With the microphone in my hand, I caught a glimpse of something white passing my periphery. I instinctively pulled back on the stick but a big bird had struck the landing gear folding area on the right wing. The impact created a hole that was filled with bird remains, bones, and feathers.

Approaching the Wichita field at 1,000 feet AGL, I called the tower and asked for landing instructions. I circled the field and lowered my landing gear on the downwind leg of my approach. Checking the landing gear lock down indicators, the right gear was not locked down!

I told the Wichita tower I might have a problem. I asked to do a fly by so they could confirm the position of my landing gear. In a few minutes, they confirmed my right landing gear was only part of the way down.

I returned to the 1,000-foot traffic pattern, cycling my landing gear. Circling the airport, I recycled the landing gear three more times. The right landing gear lock down indicator still refused to show "locked down."

I requested the tower for another fly by. Permission was granted. The Wichita tower confirmed the right gear was still not completely down. I retracted my landing gear again, telling the tower I planned to climb to 5,000 feet, enter a standard dive-bombing run, then during pull out, drop the gear. This might apply enough Gs to forcibly lock the gear fully down. If this failed to work, I would bring it in on one wheel.

At 5,000 feet I opened my dive flaps and started my dive. I started the pull out at 3,000 feet, as my speed reduced to the published landing gear extension speed, I lowered the landing gear handle. At that speed, the plane became "nose heavy," but stayed straight. As my vision returned from gray to normal, I could see the right lock down indicator was still not showing locked down.

I asked the tower for one more fly by for observation. The controller said the right gear appeared to be completely down.

I told them the indication in the cockpit was still not locked down and I would bring it in because I was getting low on fuel. The tower advised I circle the field twice while the fire trucks and meat wagons got to the runway.

In a few minutes, I was cleared to land. I kept it on the left landing gear for as long as I could. I fully expected the right gear to collapse. When the right gear touched down, it held up!

I requested a tow tractor. The next hour was spent digging the remains of the big white bird out of the hole. The leading edge was ready for repair.

I flew to Fort Worth later that afternoon. Just before sunrise the next morning, I was flying to El Paso. Again.

Dumb Things Navy Pilots
Should Never Do

There was a time when twelve Marine pilots were transferred to our VRF-2 squadron. They had been fighting in the South Pacific and were rotated back to help us deliver airplanes. Our operations officer, Rod Moore, assigned twenty pilots to ride to Montreal, Quebec, Canada in our R4D (DC-3) transport plane. Each of us was to bring back SB2C dive bombers that were manufactured there. I was given three of the new Marines as wingmen for the return flight. I told Marine Captain Rasmussen to lead our group back to our Ohio base where guns would be installed on the dive bombers. We took off and joined up heading south, southwest. The three Marines flew in formation and I flew loose on the right side. They were on the correct heading so I relaxed. Our instructions were to fly along the radio airways, which meant all day long we received Morse Code, *da dit* or *dit da*, depending on which side of the radio beam we were flying. On that day, I switched over to the commercial band frequency and listened to music.

Several hours went by. The sun was getting low in the west. Just then Captain Rasmussen radioed he was lost. I switched from the commercial band to the Columbus radio range and immediately crossed a radio beam. Should I turn west or turn east? We were down to 1,500 feet above the ground and flew over a small town with Johnstown painted on one of the buildings. I checked my gas supply and found I only had 50 gallons to get the 32 miles to Columbus.

I looked around and there was a B-17, a four-engine bomber, flying several thousand feet above us in the opposite general direction of east, northeast. I knew the Army usually practiced on the northeast radio leg, so I turned west with my flight. In four minutes, I spotted the field beacon light of our base. I picked up my mic and requested a straight in approach and split formation landing. Permission was granted. Captain Rasmussen and I landed long, leaving the other pilots landing short on the runway. Second Lt. Anderson's engine died as he landed. He required a tow tractor to tow him in.

The moral of the story is: You cannot assume experienced combat pilots can navigate correctly!

Emergency Landing in Port Columbus

Lt. Penniman and I were lucky enough to take two Grumman TBM war veteran torpedo bombers from California to Norfolk, VA.

Both planes were using a lot of oil. We had gotten to Abilene, TX for the night so we sent the RON message to our home base.

The weather had been bad to the east all morning. Bud and I had lunch by pooling our funds. We shared one bowl of chili at a cost of twenty-five cents. That was all the money we had to our names.

File photograph of a Grumman TBM Avenger

Bub Penniman and I each had a "used" TBM to return to the factory. We were both forced down at our home base in Columbus, Ohio. Neither airplane flew again—both needed new engines, and it was too late in the war to repair them. This was my last forced landing.

We knew if we could get to Vichy, MO, the colonel would loan us some money or feed us. About 3:30 p.m., the weather opened up so we flew to Vichy.

We arrived just before dark, very low on oil and gas. We met the colonel who was glad to feed us. A mechanic interrupted our meal with a discovery about our engines. He said they both had a few loose cylinders.

Each engine was a fourteen-cylinder radial, air cooled, 1,750 horsepower Wright R-2600-8 Cyclone. The engines carried 19 gallons of oil each. It seemed only reasonable to tighten them up and safety wire them.

Bud and I had breakfast with the colonel before we climbed into our torpedo bombers, amended our flight plan, and proceeded to our home base in Port Columbus.

We had just passed the Dayton Ohio Army Base when the trouble began. We decided we could make it into Columbus.

Bud's TBM was blowing oil all over; my plane had a hole in the cowling and was running rough.

We called the VRF-2 tower and explained our emergency. They cleared out all the traffic in the traffic pattern.

The fire trucks and ambulances were waiting for us.

We landed safely. Those two engines were completely worn out.

Not Too Smart

Taking an SB2C dive bomber to San Diego Naval Air Station yielded certain days of routine boredom. One hot summer afternoon, the Air Force was using the area west of El Paso for training. On this day, they had twelve B-17s flying in loose formation of threes. One Bell P-39 was making gunnery runs on them.

I was flying about 16,000 feet watching them when the thought occurred to me that maybe the P-39 pilot could use a little help. I rolled the SB2C over on its back to do a split S. The damn thing went straight down and would not pull out. The stick froze! I glanced at the airspeed, 440 knots! I thought about bailing out, but visualized getting caught on the big rudder of the tail. Naturally, I had the throttle idling. It appeared to me that there was only one hope. I rolled the elevator trim tab clear back while applying a steady pull on the stick. (I had heard that it was possible to break the control cable if you pulled the control stick too hard.) The airspeed was over 510 knots, and I was losing altitude fast.

The SB2C began to respond to my flight control imputs; the nose was coming up! I do not know how far above the ground I was when it finally leveled out, but somewhere near a few hundred feet AGL.

The first thing I did was to thank God. The second thing was to wipe the sweat from my face. The third was to get back the altitude I had lost.

After delivering the SB2C to the San Diego Naval Air Station, I returned to Columbus. The evening I returned, the main conversation at the BOQ bar was that Curtiss-Wright had offered $15,000 to their test pilots to dive the SB2Cs at 500 knots. They had turned down the opportunity. They made the same offer to us Navy pilots. All the pilots seemed to think it could not be done. When I walked in, I told the guys what I had done and explained how to bring an SB2C out of a 500-knot dive. I lost the $15,000 offer.

Hometown Buzz

A small group of us were periodically sent up to Fort Williams, Ontario, Canada (now Thunder Bay), to fly back with their SCWs (like our SB2Cs) that were made there. Canadians always had higher quality airplanes. Their planes had fewer problems and were 10 knots faster at the same throttle setting than the U.S. produced aircraft. Bill Conklin, Paul Ernsberger, and I each took off heading for Minneapolis. It was getting late, so we refueled and stayed overnight. Paul suggested two of us fly over northeast Iowa, while Bill flew the airways reporting in for all three of us heading for Chicago and Ohio. I phoned my mother that evening saying we might be flying over town tomorrow.

My folks lived about a mile north of Oelwein. I circled over their farmstead, taking some leaves out of a tree top. With Paul flying wing on me, we roared down main street Oelwein. Just for fun, I dropped my prop pitch into low range to make the ground shake. Apparently, Paul also put his in low range and the result on the ground was the burglar alarm in the bank was set off. My Uncle Clyde farmed five miles east of town. Uncle Clyde always wore a white baseball type cap. There he was, in the field pulling a disk behind his tractor. We took his cap off by flying low over him. Paul and I flew easterly, catching up with Bill Conklin. We all landed at the VRF-2 base in Columbus.

A couple of weeks later, my mother sent me a newspaper clipping. "Local boy buzzes hometown setting off burglar alarm." If the Navy knew this, we would be busted. Several weeks later my mother sent another clipping. "Local boy buzzes hometown with a B-17. Many windows broken."

The moral of this story is, don't buzz your hometown.

Instruments

It seemed like only a few of us spent time in Link Instrument Training, flew the SNJ under the hood with an instructor, and practiced instrument flying. I practiced because it looked like very cheap life insurance.

File photograph of a North American SNJ Texan

One winter, the weather was so bad that even the birds were not flying. We had days of freezing rain, rain, mist, fog, drizzle with low overcast skies. Apparently, our operations officer had received word that an aircraft carrier at Norfolk, VA needed SB2Cs immediately.

Our VRF-2 squadron had several transport planes. The biggest transport was the R4D, but it was slow. The twin engine Beechcraft held seven passengers and was much faster. Six of us instrument rated pilots were called together.

File photograph of a Douglas R4D

I had probably 100 hours as a passenger in the R4D, primarily from the 14-hour flight from San Diego to Columbus, Ohio. I flew as co-pilot a few times.

Our mission was to fly SB2Cs to Norfolk. We were to take off on instruments, fly on instruments, and land on instruments.

Two transport pilots would follow us with the Beechcraft, pick us up and fly us back on instruments. They had sandwiches, drinking water and blankets on board for our return trip. We made three round trips when the weather got better.

File photograph of a Twin Beech

Coming back to Columbus the last time our pilot, Big Mac, lost an engine. We all grabbed our parachutes and strapped them on. It was night, and we were ready to bail out. But Mac said to hold still, as he thought we might make it. Columbus tower cleared him for a straight in approach. There was little visibility with a low ceiling. Thanks to Big Mac, we made it in an airplane with one engine fully operational. Normally, a fully loaded airplane with only one operational could not maintain altitude. Both engines were replaced the next day.

The first few weeks in the Navy, my father, who served in France during WWI, wrote a very important letter to me. He said, "Son, be sure to do everything you are told. Never, ever, think about going AWOL." I had always followed his advice or orders. Except for an Army captain in Deming.

Busted

Bud Penniman and I were asked to deliver two TD2Cs to Santa Ana, CA. We were two days behind a group of eleven VRF-2 pilots also flying TD2Cs.

Because of our short range, we always refueled at Deming, NM. Deming was an Army base northwest of El Paso with mostly multi-engine aircraft operating from there. If we took on a full fuel load at Deming, we could make it to Tucson, AZ for more fuel.

Bud and I landed our TD2Cs at Deming and taxied up to the service area for fuel. We walked into flight operations and filed a flight plan for Tucson. A new Army Captain refused to sign our flight plans unless we each purchased airway maps from him for twenty-five cents each. We assured him we already had our maps. He told us he had to see them and draw a line on the maps from Deming to Tucson so we would not get lost.

We told him we had been through here many times, that we were experienced Naval Aviators from a ferry squadron, and that we would not get lost. He was not listening. We asked him to walk out to our planes with us. We could show him our maps then he could draw his silly line. He said it was too hot for him to walk out there. He liked his air-conditioned office. I told him it might be too hot for us to walk out there and back to show him our maps. That's when he started calling us four-letter words, and Bud told him he could put his maps where the sun doesn't shine.

We proceeded out to our planes once they were gassed up. We climbed in and taxied out to the end of the active runway. There were no planes in the traffic pattern. We pulled out onto the runway for takeoff. Still no planes in the pattern. The tower gave us a red light. I looked at Bud; he pointed forward, so we took off.

We arrived back in Columbus a couple of days later. We were told to see Commanding Officer Peterson. Peterson told us we had not acted like officers and gentlemen. He said we were busted! He did not ask what had really happened.

We were demoted to wing men for about two weeks. Commander Peterson called me in and wanted to know if I wanted my lead pilot authority back.

"No," I said. "I like it this way. No responsibility, no hurrying, just take it very easy." He said, "That's the problem. Everyone is taking it easy."

I told him maybe he had made a mistake by busting us. Our first CO, Johnny Rembert, would at least have asked what happened. I explained that two days before Bud and I arrived in Deming, the other eleven VRF-2 pilots had really stirred up the Army captain, but there were too many of them for the captain to lie about. Commander Peterson stood up and handed us back our lead cards.

St. Simons Island

St. Simons Island is off the coast of Georgia. I never knew there was a Navy base and airport there until I was assigned to deliver an airplane. In order for me to return to the mainland to catch one of the airlines required that I flew co-pilot in a twin-engine Grumman Goose seaplane for a whole twenty minutes. Getting out of the large aircraft, I asked the pilot if he was planning on flying back solo. "Oh, yes," he said. I wished him good luck.

File photograph of a Grumman Goose

I sat in the co-pilot seat for about twenty minutes; this led me into the single tail B-24 then the solo flight in the B-25 (PBJ).

Solo in a B-25

I returned to Columbus, Ohio for my next assignment. I slept most of the way on a DC-3 airliner.

The ferry flight to St. Simons Island was a much-appreciated break. Immediately, I was back ferrying SB2Cs from the factory to San Diego, following a tried and proven route. In early 1944, I had landed an SB2C at the El Paso airport. At that time, the runway was in much needed repair. Having been trained in making tail down three-point landings, I had stuck my dive bomber's tail wheel into a pot hole on the runway. It is difficult to taxi up to the service area without a tail wheel. I was forced to leave my SB2C at El Paso for repairs.

Each time I refueled in El Paso, I would check on the repair status of that dive bomber. Several months went by when I was finally told my SB2C dive bomber would be repaired for tomorrow. I delivered the SB2C to San Diego Naval Air Station and returned the next day. Arriving in El Paso, I was told by our local Navy liaison officer that the plane was not all done yet.

And he had a Navy full commander pilot waiting for me. We walked into the ready room and I was introduced to him. He asked if I had ever flown a multi-engine airplane. I told him "Yes, but not very much." He said that was good enough for him because he needed a co-pilot. I looked at our liaison officer. He said I would have time for the flight to Phoenix. Agreeing to be his co-pilot is when I found the plane was a four-engine, single tail B-24. The commander said we were going to Litchfield Park, which was west of

Phoenix. It was an experimental secret field for modifying certain airplanes. He explained that his co-pilot had gotten sick the night before and had ended up in the hospital. Gathering up the rest of his crew, we were hauled out to the big bird. Carrying my parachute bag plus my little change of clothes bag, I followed the commander up into the bomber. He took the left seat and motioned me into the right seat in the front cockpit area. Following a printed checklist, we walked down through each item. Finally he started the engines. I was ordered to do the radio clearances to the takeoff runway. All the engines checked out good on the rev-up. We were given permission to take off.

My impression was it took a long time to get that aircraft off the runway. Getting up to altitude, the commander explained how to handle the controls if we lost an engine. Having said that he pulled back engine number four and said, "You got it."

It seemed like I had to stand on the left rudder while adjusting the remaining three engines' power and rpm. Then I trimmed up the trim tabs. It took a bunch of muscle on the yoke to control the plane compared to the Corsair fighter plane. The commander then pushed the number four engine back up to power. This required resetting all the engine throttles and the trim tabs again. I had just gotten that done when the commander pulled the number two engine throttle back, forcing me to do the whole program over again. I glanced over at the commander. He just sat there with a smile on his face when he pushed the number two engine back up to power, allowing me to readjust everything again. By that time he said we were getting close to his landing field so he would take over. He made a nice smooth landing. After parking it, we all climbed out and climbed into a waiting truck.

At Litchfield Park headquarters, the commander and I put our equipment in his office. He sat down behind his desk and starting talking to someone on the phone. Hanging up the phone he said, "Let's get something to eat."

During our meal, the commander mentioned one of the things they were doing there was converting B-25s into night fighters. Equipped with the newest radar, their longer range and more guns, they would be useful in the Pacific. As I was absorbing his facts; he said he had a B-25 at the Kansas City airport waiting for me to bring to Litchfield Park. Me? I'm still supposed to take that repaired SB2C to the San Diego Naval Air Station.

He smiled and said that's who he had been talking to on the phone. It was not done yet. He said he understood I carried a TR book (Transportation Request) which is like a government check book for the commercial flight to Kansas City. I replied I had a TR book. The commander had a room arranged for me at their little BOQ (Bachelor Officers Quarters). He would have a staff car take me to Phoenix airport in the morning. I asked about a co-pilot. He said there was a Navy mechanic with the airplane and he would help with that and changing the fuel tanks that are unreachable for the pilot.

I had breakfast with the commander the next morning. He handed me the operating manual for the B-25 and smiled again. He suggested I would have time to read it because it was going to take almost all day to get to Kansas City. The staff car was waiting for me outside. As I was thanking the commander for breakfast, he told me I had to have that B-25 here in Litchfield Park by tomorrow evening to complete their contract!

File photograph of a North American PBJ

After my B-24 "training flight," I was told to go commercial airlines from Arizona to Kansas City, and bring back a B-25—a PBJ—to Arizona's "Litchfield Park." I flew it solo from Kansas City to Fort Worth. At Fort Worth, the airport was under instrument conditions, and a B-26 pilot was solo in the instrument stack. The tower finally let him come in with me right behind him. He was so happy I had been able to help him. I refueled and flew on to Litchfield Park.

A very good airplane.

I arrived in Kansas City late in the afternoon and there sat a B-25. The serial numbers checked out, so that was the one. I asked a flight line attendant where to find the Navy mechanic. He had been there, but a good-looking redheaded gal driving a car with Kansas plates had picked him up about 1745. I went back to the terminal and phoned for a cab to get a motel room near the airport. I told the cab driver I wanted picked up at 0730 to go back to the airport. After eating supper, I scanned the B-25 operating manual and fell asleep.

After breakfast, the cab arrived to take me to the airport. Putting my bag, parachute and airway maps in the B-25, I slowly walked around it doing the preflight inspection. An Army man drove up asking if I needed some help. I told him I would in a short hour because I was waiting for a Navy mechanic to arrive to go with me. 0900 arrived and still no Navy mechanic. I remembered the commander had ordered me to have this B-25 in Litchfield

Park by evening. The Army person came back. He stood by with fire extinguishers while I started the engines. I received taxi instructions from the tower and checked my engines before takeoff. I was cleared for takeoff for Fort Worth. My thinking was, maybe I could pick up a co-pilot at Fort Worth while refueling.

Before I got to Oklahoma City, the weather turned worse. I put it on automatic pilot so I could change the fuel tanks for landing in Fort Worth. Making an instrument landing required skill, training, and an instrument rating, which I had. Calling Fort Worth on the radio, I was given number five in the instrument stack. I followed the tower's instructions on altitude step downs and waited.

I heard a pilot in a B-26 (a hot medium bomber with twin engines) requesting emergency landing instructions because he had fifty gallons of fuel left and was flying solo. The tower said no because it was impossible for him to be flying a B-26 solo. I picked up my mic, identified myself and told them I was also a "B-25 solo" with plenty of fuel. They let the B-26 pilot in with me following right behind him. I was sure the men in the tower had a hard time believing each of us were solo.

I topped off all my fuel tanks. There were no VRF-2 planes in the service area. I checked the ready room, but no one was there. I told the B-26 pilot I had to go shortly to obey my orders. He thought he would stay over in Fort Worth until tomorrow. I filed a flight plan for Litchfield Park and took off.

I arrived in Litchfield Park before dark. The commander was waiting for me in his Jeep. I explained I had hated to leave the mechanic, but I needed to get here according to his instructions. We ate supper together after I returned his operating manual for the B-25. He thanked me for the help and said my SB2C was ready to fly. The same room was ready for me that night. He would have the same staff car and driver take me to the Phoenix airport in the morning so I could fly commercial to El Paso. The commander got really serious. Looking me straight in the eyes he said, "What we are doing here is very secret. Do not log these flights and tell no one." He said the Navy liaison officer had been reporting me RON every night in El Paso.

Late the next morning, I arrived in El Paso and talked to our Navy liaison officer. I climbed into the repaired SB2C and flew it to the San Diego Naval Air Station. What an experience. Several weeks later, I was assigned as co-pilot in a B-25 from Tulsa to the east coast; I never said a single word about B-25s.

Fourth of July 1944

On July 4, 1944 Ensign Bud Penniman and I were asked to deliver Corsairs. As we walked out towards our Corsairs, we decided to give the civilians an airshow over the Buckeye Lake resort area. Over Buckeye Lake, we did the usual loops, snaps, inside spins, and so on. As we climbed back up to 10,000 feet, Bud said he wondered what it was like to do an outside spin. Typically, in a spin, the cockpit is on the inside of the circle that the plane makes when spinning. I told Bud I would try it. Putting that nice airplane into a full stall, I pushed the stick full forward, full right rudder. I think I did one full spin; my seat belt and shoulder straps were hurting from the pressure as I reversed the controls. My eyes were getting red when the Corsair came out of the outside spin. I was at about 1,500 feet of altitude. Bud radioed asking, "How was it?"

"Don't do it." I told him. "It was terrible." No wonder they do not teach us both kinds of spins in flight training.

The moral of the story is, never do outside spins. Most planes would crumble, and they don't help a pilot's body either.

Clueless in Nashville

By late 1944, I had been promoted up to a "lead pilot." Ron Moore "assigned" me to lead two Marine pilots all three of us flying new SB2C dive bombers. The weather was marginal, but we made the delivery, turned over the log books for each airplane. We were to ride back to Port Columbus, but in order to do so required us to transfer to another airline at Nashville, TN.

I had written a government check to pay for our airline seats, for I was the one who carried the Transportation Request (TR) check book for the three of us. There was little rest for ferry pilots as we were still very active supporting the war effort, and we also had priority in airline seats. As we waited for the plane to arrive so we could return to Port Columbus, we were told it was full. Which meant airline personnel had the unpleasant duty of "bumping" passengers for us to return to duty.

We were patient as the airline indicated that three of the passengers already aboard the airplane needed to get off for us. We were surprised that the three passengers who got off were from Hollywood, CA: Veronica Lake, Danny Kaye, and George Goebel. They were flying to New York to put on a USO show for the military. George Goebel was extremely vocal, telling us we could wait because they were very important. I tried to tell George that we were just following our orders. I am very sure that George never really understood that the men feeding the aircraft carriers with new combat aircraft had a better priority than entertainers.

I was already aboard the airliner when I realized I never asked when the next airline flight could take the movie stars to their USO show.

Number 13

While in flight training at Pensacola, I was assigned plane number 13. My trainer asked if I might be sick or not feeling up to it. Not knowing the difference, I took the training flight and got an up check (I passed). Some people believe the number 13 is bad luck. It must be an attitude thing.

Do not believe everything you hear in aviation.

Marine Lt. Anderson and I had been roommates at Pensacola for approximately three weeks. We had both received our gold wings the same day at Pensacola. His dad was a Marine officer and he wished to be a Marine pilot. I was so pleased to see him again when he joined our VRF-2 squadron. Lt. Anderson was sitting in our ready room when I returned from a delivery flight. I sat down beside him and asked, "Why the gloom?"

He said, "Have you heard that we just lost another Marine pilot?"

No, I had not. That made four in five weeks.

He said his squadron only had one plane shot down in combat in the South Pacific, and they had rescued the pilot.

Not knowing what else to say, I told Andy to come with me. I had to turn in my flight time downstairs at the log room.

The guys pulled my log book and Andy asked them to pull his log book too. My log showed over 1,500 solo hours and Andy's had just a little over 500 solo hours. I told Andy that I felt Marines had more and better flight experience than we did. He said they never went up if the weather was less than perfect.

He said, "You guys are going up in almost everything." Then he added that the war weary planes we flew back for major overhaul were nothing but pieces of junk. He said he could understand why I had 13 forced landings and he had none.

And there are reasons for pilots to keep up their instrument rating.

One Dear John

Arriving back to our VRF-2 squadron base in late February 1945, I had a letter waiting for me. I had been writing to a girl about once a week for close to two years.

I opened the letter and it read, "Dear Ralph, I have been seeing another person each weekend for two months. I have only seen you once in two years. I will not be writing you anymore." Signed Jean.

I felt rejected and betrayed at the same time. My good friend and flying buddy Paul Ernsberger walked into the pilot's ready room and sat down beside me. His question was, "Why the long face?"

I replied that I just received a "Dear John letter!"

Paul thought awhile. He put his hand on my shoulder and said, "Well, maybe it's not so bad. Maybe you might be better off."

I could not understand how.

Just then we were assigned flights; Paul to Norfolk and I was assigned a flight to Oakland, CA.

A few days later I arrived back at Port Columbus at about 1600 hours. A note was in my mailbox from Paul to call their apartment in Westerville, OH. I made the phone call from our main hangar. Paul's wife Meriam answered. She said Paul was taking a shower and that she had some extra pork chops. She wanted me to come for dinner. She said Paul would drive down to get me in about an hour. I agreed, thanked her, and hung up.

I hurried to the Bachelor Officers Quarters to clean up and get into fresh clothes. Paul arrived on time. Driving to their apartment in Westerville, we talked about our flights and the weather. Paul mentioned they had a surprise for me as we parked. He tooted his horn as he got out, then he chuckled.

Meriam was waiting for us at their door. I thanked her for the invitation because it had been a long time since I enjoyed a home cooked meal.

As we walked towards the dining room, Meriam said, "Paul and I have something else you might like."

In the doorway, with an apron on, stood one of the cutest little gals I had ever seen! Meriam picked up the conversation saying, "Ralph Alshouse, I would like you to meet Mary Morgan."

My whole life started changing for the better right then.

Lieutenant Junior Grade Ralph Alshouse

The Whiskey Experience

Our Navy VRF-2 squadron had many shortages during WWII. One particular shortage was good ground crew personnel.

During March or April 1944, the Navy called a retired chief petty officer back into active duty. In the Navy's wisdom, they assigned him to be in charge of our entire ground crew. He had the great ability of handling young men fairly.

Approximately two weeks following his arrival, I received a note from the chief in my small mailbox. (This was our internal method of communication.) The chief requested I stop at his office in one of our aircraft hangars. Arriving at his office doorway, the chief stood up smiling and shook my hand. Our first meeting. He poured a cup of black coffee for each of us and motioned for me to sit near his desk. The coffee was so strong, I believed the spoon would have stood straight up in it.

He opened the conversation by saying, "My research tells me you do not belong to the officers wine mess." I agreed with him because I had just come off a farm, had not been to college, and lacked the experience of being a responsible drinker. He explained his crew was young and many of them were alcohol abusers. If he could get a steady supply of whiskey, he could ration it out to them, keeping them under control. He then suggested I join the wine mess, getting four to six quarts of whiskey each month, and give it to him so he could ration it out. I agreed to this.

Every month I would take my smaller Navy suitcase, purchase my allotment of whiskey, put it in the suitcase and take it to the chief. Everything worked out great. We had the best ground crew.

I had purchased a used 1936 Ford car a few weeks after I received my Dear John letter. While I was out on a delivery flight, the ground crew would use it. I expected the gas tank to be full when I got back each time. As mechanics, they kept it in good mechanical shape.

Our arrangement worked perfectly for many months until I returned from a lengthy flight one evening. The next morning after breakfast I paid for and filled my suitcase with whiskey. I had just gotten near the hangar when an announcement came over the loud speaker system said, "Alshouse, you've got an immediate flight to San Diego with an SB2C. It will be one of the last ones to fill a carrier. You will leave now!"

I put the suitcase with the whiskey in my locker, pulled out my parachute and flight gear and locked the locker. Someone brought me the log books as I climbed into the assigned SB2C. I fired it up and headed west.

I returned a couple of days later on an airline arriving about 0200. The chief was waiting for me with a long face as I got off the airliner. We both walked over to our hangar while chief explained we had a problem. The problem was our entire ground crew was in the Brig (jail).

As we walked into the hangar, I told him I had more whiskey for him. I unlocked my locker, pulled out the suitcase to give it to the chief. It was empty! He said, "That's what happened."

We looked and saw that the crew members had pulled the pins on the hinges, taken the whiskey and put the pins back in. During their party, they had busted up a bunch of stuff, and the skipper was really mad.

The chief said I should talk to the skipper at 0800. It was now about 0300. At 0800, I was explaining to our grumpy skipper how we had been operating and how well it worked. As a squadron, we were nothing with these guys in the Brig. I suggested he confine them to the field, allowing them back to work. He said he would if I stopped supplying the whiskey to the chief. After I agreed, he wrote an order restricting them to the base and releasing them from the brig. We walked over to the brig, handed the order to the officer in charge. Together we all walked back to the hangar. Nearing his office, the chief stopped, turned and gave them the riot act. He was so sincere that even I had tears in my eyes.

He was such a wonderful person and well respected. He later got influenza and was in the base hospital. The hospital had to establish a rule that only two could be his room at one time. I had to wait in line to see him. We needed more people like him.

Last Flight

The last aircraft I flew as an active-duty pilot was the Lockheed R50.

File photograph of a Lockheed R50

The mission was to pick up and deliver a senior officer from Detroit, MI to Washington, DC and then return to Port Columbus after dark. We were delayed several hours leaving Washington.

The delay affected my new wife significantly. Even though I had delivered hundreds of aircraft for the war effort, my wife was convinced we had crashed.

POSTFLIGHT

Scope

The scope of our work toward the war effort, all of the Navy's ferry pilots production was captured in this photograph of hundreds of new naval aircraft staged in a blimp hangar in Santa Ana, CA before being loaded or flown aboard new aircraft carriers being delivered from naval shipyards.

File photograph of the inside of a hangar
at Naval Air Station Santa Ana

Happiness

Most people just think they know what happiness is when they lack experience and understanding on how to capture actual, complete, real happiness!

We have to go back in time to WW II and airplanes. All Navy great airplanes in that day and age had Round Engines. Big Round Engines, some of them delivered 2,000 horsepower.

Standard safety procedure for a pilot to start one Round Engine was to have two ground crew members, each with large, tall fire extinguisher on a narrow 2-wheel hand cart, standing on each side of your engine, just ahead of the plane's wing. Remember each of these two ground crew members is just as important as the pilot is, because the pilot is nothing without them!

Assuming the pilot has checked the 120 octane fuel tanks for fullness, and the fuel caps are all on properly, that the elevator, aileron locking blocks are removed, that the air speed sock has been removed, and the wheel chocks are in place. The pilot is now ready to mount the mighty bird by climbing up into the cockpit with a parachute buckled on, and sit down on the packed chute.

The pilot is now ready to test his skill and training by making absolutely certain the main engine switch is OFF. The pilot signals the ground crew to prepare the beautiful engine for start by pulling each of the four propeller blades counterclockwise. Rotation of the propeller usually requires both men on a cold day. This eliminates most of the crankcase oil from the bottom cylinders that collected overnight.

The pilot advances the throttle just above idle speed, primes the engine one full push on the gasoline primer on a typical day, two pushes on a chilly day and three pushes on a cold day. Turn the main engine switch completely on (both magnetos), sticks his head out the side of the cockpit, yells loudly, "ALL CLEAR?" If no one is under or in front of the propeller, and each man is pointing fire extinguisher at each side of the wonderful Round Engine with his other hand on the trigger. If it is clear, they yell back, all clear.

The pilot engages the starter, and the big blades begin to turn. The Round Engine growls, grunts, farts a couple times, two or three of the cylinders ignite, the propeller turns a little faster, 120 octane gasoline and flames are spitting out both sides of the engine through the exhaust. Both men on the ground are blowing CO_2 on their side of the engine suppressing the flames, smoke is rising 10-12 feet above the engine, more cylinders are firing, the propeller spins faster, flames stop coming out of both sides, the ground crew smiles, the big Round Engine warms up and begins to purr, then settles in a quiet roar of all eighteen big cylinders.

This is absolute happiness, it is much better than a big juicy steak dinner, or even sex.

The skilled team has accomplished something useful with the Round Engine ready to defend our country and advance freedom. Freedom is not free.

In Closing....

I am a little like that famous baseball player who said, "If I had known I was going to live this long, I would have taken better care of myself." With that said, I am pleased to be over 99 years old and still counting. Looking back, I might have done a few things differently, but at the time, it was the best decision with the information available.

I have no desire to go back in years or be younger. I refuse to go through several terrible experiences again. Once was enough.

My days earning Navy Wings of Gold and being part of a VRF-2 squadron were wonderful accomplishments in WWII. After the war, my squadron mates attended reunions. We originally met every five years, then we met every two years. Then, with declining numbers, we would meet every year. Our last reunion was in Pensacola, in April 2005. During those days, any day could have been our last day. For many pilots in WWII, their last flight was their last day on earth.

Flight Summary

1. Enlisted in U.S. Navy in August 1942 as seaman second, 18 years old. 5 men signed up, 3 accepted into Cadet (V5) training.

2. Transferred to Cadets (V5) September 1942. Sent to Eagle Grove Junior College, Iowa for ground school classes and flight training at Clarion airport. Soloed on 10-8-1942, with 2.4 hours of flight instruction.

3. January 1943, sent to pre-flight training at the University of Iowa, Iowa City, Iowa. Learned to swim, won USN 150# boxing championship. 24 percent washed out for various reasons.

4. March 1943, transferred to E-Base at Wold Chamberlin Field at Minneapolis, Minnesota. Flew bi-wing "yellow pearls" (Stearmans).

5. June 1943 moved to Pensacola, Florida Naval Air Station. Final squadron training in Scout Observation single engine seaplanes used aboard Battleships and Cruisers. 10 Cadets started; 5 Cadets completed training.

6. Commissioned October 26, 1943 as Naval Aviator #P-7345. Total flight time 239. 7 hours. Received orders to report to USS Colorado.

7. Ensign Leo Nolz insisted on trading orders, approved by the U.S. Navy. Ensign Nolz died in the South Pacific at the Battle of Okinawa.

8. Sent to Naval Air Facility, Port Columbus, Ohio on November 16, 1943. Assigned to VRF-2.

9.Delivered 146 combat aircraft and was transferred to inactive duty in January 1946. Total flight time of 1657.8 hours logged.

10.Recorded 13 forced landings of which two were dead sticks: FG-3 on fire over Pittsburgh, Pennsylvania; landed in a cow pasture in Georgia; landed on a highway in Alabama; landed on a ranch in New Mexico; rime ice accumulated on the wings in Tennessee; the automatic pilot, while turned off, popped on during takeoff with a SC-1 in Abilene, Texas; forced to land because of an unexpected sand storm approaching El Paso, Texas; struck by lightning approaching Douglas, Arizona; shucking cylinders near Vichy, Missouri; forced to land at Santa Ana, California with a TD2C when the field was closed to instrument landings; and hit a large bird (Sandhill Crane) which prevent the landing gear from extending going into Wichita, KS; after several cyclings of the landing gear that the control tower confirmed to be a partial extension, low on fuel and cycled the gear one more time the control tower said the gear appeared to be down and locked, landed with an unsafe landing gear indication without incident.

11.Met a F6F fighter while landing at San Pedro, California, NAS. With very limited visibility, I landed with tower instructions and he landed according to the wind TEE. We met near the center length of the runway, each reacted as on a highway (swing to the right). We missed by inches.

12.Damaged three aircraft: pulled the tail wheel out of an SB2C dive bomber in a pothole on the El Paso, Texas runway. Hit a large bird over Kansas, causing damage to the right wing of an SB2C at the folded landing gear area, preventing full landing gear extension. Bent an SB2C empennage over Virginia, practicing high speed stalls at 275 knots.

13. Learned the scary way how to pull a dive bomber out of a dive at a speed over 500 knots. (Stick freezes at 440 knots). Used elevator trim tabs, a steady pull on the stick. I briefed my squadron mates, do not do a split-S with an SB2C dive bomber!

14. Did an outside spin over Buckeye Lake with an FG Corsair fighter, Bud Penniman and I were assigned to check out in them on July 4th 1944. Not a good maneuver for air shows. It's very painful on shoulder straps and seat belt, plus red eyes with dark red eyesight. No wonder they do not teach outside spins in flight training.

15. Flew co-pilot on a B-24 single tail fin, from El Paso, Texas to Phoenix, Arizona. Flew a B-25 solo from Kansas City to Phoenix, for night fighter modifications.

16. Assigned to fly over 28 types of Naval Aircraft: from the smallest, a Cub ambulance, to the biggest a B-24, to the fastest single-seat aircraft, a Corsair.

17. Won VFR-2 high man of all pilot's award in June 1945.

18. Returned to NAS Columbus, Ohio October 5, 1949 for a needed refresher in flying. Received a letter of promotion to Full Lt.

19. Received a letter inviting a return to active duty for Korea. Turned it down because I was farming. My brother went to Korea in a Marine tank unit. I joined the U.S. Navy Reserves.

20. July 28, 1960 received an honorable discharge from U.S. Navy.

History of VRF-2

Prepared April 2004 for:

Annette Fromm, Folklore Society, Miami, Florida
The American Veterans History Project, Library of Congress
Nancy Mitchell, coordinator, Library of Congress

VRF-2, formed December 1, 1943, was one of three test and delivery squadrons identified with the Naval Air Transport Service. It replaced the Aircraft Delivery Unit based at Port Columbus, Ohio.

The mission identified for VRF-2 was to test and then deliver Navy operational aircraft, produced in the Midwest (states) and Canada, to destinations and ports of embarkation on the East and West coasts.

The SB2C Helldiver was manufactured at Curtiss-Wright, Columbus and at Montreal (Canadian Car & Foundry) and Fort Williams, Canada. 5,105 at Curtiss-Wright, 894 at Montreal, and 300 at Fort Williams.

The FG Corsair was manufactured at the Goodyear plant in Akron, Ohio. Of the 3,808 produced by Goodyear, 2,012 were delivered to the British Royal Navy under the Lend-Lease Act. The British aircraft had six inches taken off their wing tips for the English aircraft carriers.

VRF-2 pilots logged major hours in the SB2C Helldivers and FG Corsairs.

A routine assignment would start with a group of eight or ten pilots flying the FG Corsairs (for Royal Navy) from Columbus to Roosevelt Field, New York. Complete the paperwork at operations, get aboard a Navy bus for the short ride to Floyd Bennett Field, where the VRF-2 R4D transport would wait to take the ferry pilots back to Columbus, arriving in the late afternoon. Check the assignment board and it would have many of these same pilots assigned the next day to another SB2C or FG destined for the West coast. After one overnight stop, we would land at San Diego or Alameda, and several hours later, get aboard a NATS (Naval Air Transport Service) transport heading East. Spend the night on the transport, arriving at Port Columbus about noon. A normal month for a VRF-2 pilot would have him on the West coast three or four times. Mixed in with the schedule would be another to the East coast, a regular transport ride to Montreal or Minneapolis to fly back the SBWs and SBFs manufactured in Canada.

Being assigned in San Diego to deliver a Navy plane to an East coast base was not unusual.

File photograph of a Curtiss SBW

This Canadian aircraft was consistently delivered without bugs; U.S. manufactured aircraft of the same type consistently had bugs. SBWs were faster than the U.S.-manufactured aircraft.

Navy Pilot, F-18 (2009)

Son Mike and his wife Jenny lived in Virginia Beach, VA. This is part of Norfolk and Ocean Side large Naval base complex. They are blessed with three squadrons of Navy pilots flying the latest F-18 planes. They are rotated on and off the nuclear carriers as needed. Most all their flying is at night!

Jenny was cutting an F-18 pilot's hair. She mentioned her father-in-law flew Corsairs and several other Navy planes in WWII. He had 13 forced landings and is still alive today.

The F-18 fighter pilot reached over on his left shoulder, pulled off his squadron identification patch and handed it to Jenny and said, "Here give this to him!"

TO THOSE WHO
HAVE SERVED WITH US

I guess we who mount the cockpit
Are a different breed of men.
With a special kind of feeling
For the ones we call friend.

It's an arm around the shoulder
When the morning comes too soon,
And a late-night conversation
In a thousand hotel rooms.

11's a dead stick in Atlanta
Or a wheels-up in St. Paul.
It takes a tough old sailor
To keep going through it all.

But we're so much less than human
When we lose one of our own.
There's one more empty cockpit.
This old pilot has gone home.

My Papers

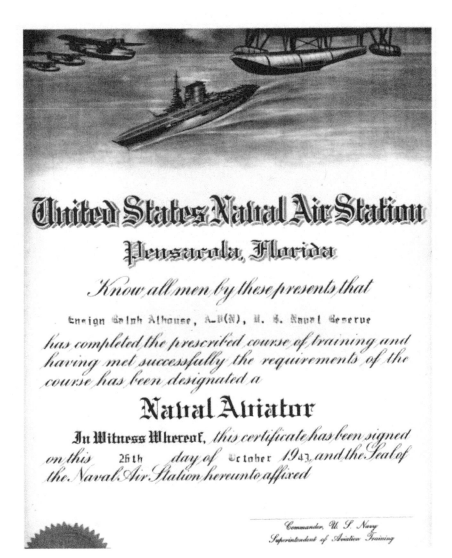

United States Naval Air Station
Pensacola, Florida

Know all men by these presents that

Ensign Ralph Alhouse, A-V(N), U. S. Naval Reserve

has completed the prescribed course of training and having met successfully the requirements of the course has been designated a

Naval Aviator

In Witness Whereof, *this certificate has been signed on this* 26th *day of* October 1943, *and the Seal of the Naval Air Station hereunto affixed*

Commander, U. S. Navy
Superintendent of Aviation Training

Ensign Alshouse Naval Aviator Designation

In reply address not the signer of this
letter, but Bureau of Naval Personnel,
Navy Department, Washington, D. C.
Refer to No. 3E0559

Pers-3176-SEK-2

NAVY DEPARTMENT

ORIGINAL

BUREAU OF NAVAL PERSONNEL

WASHINGTON, D. C.

16 December 1945.

From: The Chief of Naval Personnel.
To: Ensign Ralph Alshouse, A-V(N), USNR,

Air Ferry Squadron Two.

Via: Commanding Officer, U. S. NAVAL AIR FACILITY COLUMBUS, OHIO

PAID PER DIEM ALLOWANCE

Subject: Travel orders.

Enclosure: NO. 89595.

1.   You are hereby authorized to perform such travel from time to
time, as may be necessary for the purpose indicated below, this being in
addition to your present duties: Between Columbus, Ohio,
and such places within or outside the continental limits of the United States
as may be necessary to visit in connection with your duties as aircraft
delivery unit pilot a naval air ferry pilot.

2.   In performing the above travel, government air and/or commercial
air is directed where necessary to expedite completion of this duty.

3.   For travel by naval transport aircraft Class Two priority
is hereby certified.

4.   This authority for travel will terminate February 1, 1946.

5.   In addition to the actual cost of travel to the government,
a per diem of $6.00 in lieu of subsistence will be allowed while absent from
your station, except while occupying government quarters when a per diem of
$3.00 will be allowed.

6.   You will submit on the last day of each quarter a written report
giving the information called for by Form BNP 330.

Copy to:
Bu. Aero.

10 February

to Ensign Ralph Alshouse, A-V(N), USNR.

ORIGINAL

RANDALL JACOBS
R-3490

P-1720

Ensign Alshouse Travel Orders

Ensign Alshouse Honorable Discharge Certificate

NOTICE OF SEPARATION FROM THE U. S. NAVAL SERVICE
NAVPERS-553 (Rev. 8-45)

1. SERIAL ON FILE NO. 2. NAME (LAST) (FIRST) (MIDDLE) 3. RATE AND CLASS AND RANK AND CLASSIFICATION 4. PERMANENT ADDRESS FOR MAILING PURPOSES	5. PLACE OF SEPARATION
320559 ALSHOUSE, RALPH (N(LT JG (A-1)L USNR 1515-9 R.F.D. 2 OELWEIN, IA.	COM NINE

					6. CHARACTER OF SEPARATION

Rel from act duty under hon cond.

7. ADDRESS FROM WHICH EMPLOYMENT WILL BE SOUGHT

Same as 4.

8. RACE	9. SEX	10. MARITAL STATUS	11. U. S. CITIZEN (YES OR NO)	12. DATE AND PLACE OF BIRTH
W	M	M	Yes	12-17-23, Oelwein, Ia.

13. SELECTIVE SERVICE BOARD OF REGISTRATION / 15. HOME ADDRESS AT TIME OF ENTRY INTO SERVICE

Registered: Yes Oelwein, Ia. — Same as 4.

16. MEANS OF ENTRY INDICATE BY CHECK IN APPROPRIATE BOX	17. DATE OF ENTRY INTO ACTIVE SERVICE	18. NET SERVICE (FOR PAY PURPOSES) YRS. MOS. DAYS
☒ ENLISTED ☐ INDUCTED ☒ COMMISSIONED	1-7-43	3 0 3

DATE 8-20-42 DATE 10-26-43

19. PLACE OF ENTRY INTO ACTIVE SERVICE

Pre-Flt. Sch. M. Iowa City, Iowa

20. QUALIFICATIONS, CERTIFICATES HELD, ETC.

Nav. Avia.
Commercial Lic.

21. RATINGS HELD

23. SERVICE SCHOOLS COMPLETED / WEEKS

09 Flight Inst. (HTA)
Prim., Inter., Adv.   47

24. SERVICE (VESSELS AND STATIONS SERVED ON)

VRF-2 Columbus, O.

IMPORTANT! IF PREMIUM IS NOT PAID WHEN DUE OR WITHIN THIRTY-ONE DAYS THEREAFTER INSURANCE WILL LAPSE. MAKE CHECKS OR MONEY ORDERS PAYABLE TO THE TREASURER OF THE U. S. AND FORWARD TO COLLECTOR'S SUBDIVISION VETERANS ADMINISTRATION, WASHINGTON 25, D. C.

25. KIND OF INSURANCE	26. EFFECTIVE MONTH OF ALLOTMENT DISCONTINUANCE	27. MONTH NEXT PREMIUM DUE	28. AMOUNT OF PREMIUM DUE EACH MONTH	29. INTENTION OF VETERAN TO CONTINUE INSURANCE
N	12/45	1/46	6.50	Yes-partial

30. TOTAL PAYMENT UPON DISCHARGE	31. TRAVEL OR RELEASE ALLOWANCE INCLUDED IN TOTAL PAYMENT	32. INITIAL MUSTERING OUT PAY	33. NAME OF DISBURSING OFFICER
		$100	F.G. MATHIS LT CDR.

34. REMARKS

Amer. Thea.
WWII Vic. Med.

35. SIGNATURE (BY DIRECTION OF COMMANDING OFFICER)

E W Holzapfel

E.W. HOLZAPFEL LT CDR.

36. NAME AND ADDRESS OF LAST EMPLOYER	37. DATES OF LAST EMPLOYMENT	38. MAIN CIVILIAN OCCUPATION AND D. O. T. NO.
Student	FROM: TO:	Student

39. JOB PREFERENCE (LIST TYPE, LOCALITY, AND GENERAL AREA)	40. PREFERENCE FOR ADDITIONAL TRAINING (TYPE OF TRAINING)
Dairy supervisor	Reserve educ. agriculture

41. NON-SERVICE EDUCATION (YEARS SUCCESSFULLY COMPLETED) GRAM. 8 H. S. 4 COLL.

1-8-45   RALPH ALSHOUSE

47. DATE OF SEPARATION   48. SIGNATURE OF PERSON BEING SEPARATED

Ralph Alshouse

FILE No. 987	FILED FOR ... AND THE 28th ... DAY OF ... STATE OF IOWA, WAYNE COUNTY.
RECORDING FEE $ None	Au..st 85 1:05 JOY C. LONEY, Recorder

Ensign Alshouse Notice of Separation from the U.S. Naval Service Certificate

Acknowledgements

I owe a special debt of gratitude to Mark Hewitt, a former Naval Aviator like me, for his leadership, encouragement, and flight experience. Without Mark, this book never would have happened.

I want to send a special thank you to my daughter, Catherine Wilson, a retired award-winning teacher for her editing skills, advice, and suggestions to make this a better book. I appreciate her husband, Steve Peterson, fully supporting Cate to work her editing magic on this manuscript.

Also, I would be remiss in not crediting my dear wife, Shirley Alshouse, for all of her tremendous support as I recorded my experiences during WWII; during flight training as a Cadet, then as a pilot flight leader in VRF-2, Air Ferry Squadron 2. Her support allowed me time from farming to work on this book.

Thank you to Alyssa Palmer of Palmer Photography for the photographs of my Celestial Navigation workbook and my Logbook.

Lastly, at 99-years-old, I wonder sometimes how and/or why I am still alive today. I am indeed blessed to have such a wonderful family and great friends.

Any errors found in this TRUE novel are my total responsibility.

–Ralph T. Alshouse

About the Author

Photo credit: Steve Peterson

Ralph T. Alshouse is a retired farmer, city mayor, farm administration executive, and military pilot. He is a graduate of Iowa State University and holds a Master's degree in Public Financial Management from The American University. He served as an officer in the U.S. Navy, was designated a Naval Aviator on October 26, 1943 and was assigned to VRF-2 to test and deliver Navy operational aircraft, produced in the United States and Canada to destinations and ports of embarkation on the East and West coasts. He delivered 146 aircraft and logged 1,657.8 hours of flight time.

Note from Ralph T. Alshouse

Word-of-mouth is crucial for any author to succeed. If you enjoyed *80 Percent Luck, 20 Percent Skill,* please leave a review online—anywhere you are able. Even if it's just a sentence or two. It would make all the difference and would be very much appreciated.

Thanks!
Ralph T. Alshouse

We hope you enjoyed reading this title from:

BLACK🌹ROSE
writing™

www.blackrosewriting.com

Subscribe to our mailing list – *The Rosevine* – and receive **FREE** books, daily deals, and stay current with news about upcoming releases and our hottest authors.
Scan the QR code below to sign up.

Already a subscriber? Please accept a sincere thank you for being a fan of Black Rose Writing authors.

View other Black Rose Writing titles at
www.blackrosewriting.com/books and use promo code
PRINT to receive a **20% discount** when purchasing.